THE HEAD HUNTERS
OF
NORTHERN LUZON

Cornelis De Witt Willcox

1st WORLD
LIBRARY
Literary Society

The Head Hunters of Northern Luzon

Cornelis De Witt Willcox

© 1st World Library – Literary Society, 2005
PO Box 2211
Fairfield, IA 52556
www.1stworldlibrary.org
First Edition

LCCN: 2004195605

Softcover ISBN: 1-4218-0426-3
Hardcover ISBN: 1-4218-0326-7
eBook ISBN: 1-4218-0526-X

Purchase *"The Head Hunters of Northern Luzon"*
as a traditional bound book at:
www.1stWorldLibrary.org/purchase.asp?ISBN=1-4218-0426-3

1st World Library Literary Society is a nonprofit
organization dedicated to promoting literacy by:

- Creating a free internet library accessible from any computer worldwide.
- Hosting writing competitions and offering book publishing scholarships.

The Head Hunters of Northern Luzon
contributed by Tim, Ed & Rodney
in support of
1st World Library Literary Society

CONTENTS

PREFACE.

In 1910 the Secretary of the Interior of the Philippine Islands did me the honor to invite me to accompany him on his annual tour of inspection through the Mountain Province of Northern Luzon. In the following pages I have tried to describe what fell under my notice during the journey, with such comments, observations, and conclusions as seemed pertinent.

I should like here to thank Mr. Worcester for having invited me to join him, and Major-General Duvall, United States Army, for allowing me to accept. My thanks are also due the various officers and officials of the Insular Government who placed me under obligations by their hospitality and other courtesies and by the never-failing patience with which they received and answered my many questions. To my friend Colonel J.G. Harbord, United States Army, Assistant Director of Constabulary, I am beholden for instructions sent out in advance of the journey to the various Constabulary posts on the itinerary, directing them to offer me every opportunity to accomplish the purpose of my trip. Except where otherwise indicated, the illustrations are from photographs taken either by Mr. Worcester himself, or else under his direction. Some of these, as shown, were lent to me by the National Geographic Magazine of Washington, and others by the Bureau of Insular Affairs of the War Department.

My best thanks are due and given in each case. Dr. Heiser was kind enough to let me have a few photographs taken by him. To Lieutenant P.D. Glassford, 2d Regiment of Field Artillery, I am indebted for the map of Northern Luzon and for one or two other illustrations copied from Jenks' "The Bontoc Igorot"; to Father Malumbres, of the Dominican Monastery in Manila, for information relating to Padre Villaverde and for the portrait of that missionary; it is to be regretted that this portrait should be so unsatisfactory, but it is the only one available. The frontispiece is by Mr. Julian Miller, who has lived in the Igorot country, and whose drawing is from life.

C. De W.W.
West Point, N.Y.,
January, 1912.

CHAPTER I

Highlanders of Northern Luzon. - Meaning of the word "Igorot." - Trails. - The Mountain Province. - Nature of the country.

It is to be regretted that the people of the United States should in general show so little interest in the Philippine Islands. This lack of interest may be due to lack of knowledge; if this be so, then it is the duty of those better informed to do all that lies in their power to develop the interest now regrettably absent. Be this as it may, it is assumed here that most of our people do not know that a very large fraction of the inhabitants of the Philippines consists of the so-called wild men, and that of these the greatest group or collection is found in the mountains of Northern Luzon.

These mountaineers or highlanders constitute perhaps, all other things being equal, as interesting a body of uncivilized people as is to be found on the face of the earth to-day. The Spaniards, of course, soon discovered their existence, the first mention of them being made by De Morga, in his "*Sucesos de las Islas Filipinas*" (1609). He speaks [1] of them as inhabiting the interior of a rough mountainous country, where are "many natives who are not pacified, nor has anyone gone into their country, who call themselves Ygolotes," Here we have the first form, the classic form according to Retana, of the word now universally written *Igorrote*, or in English *Igorot.* The word itself means "highlanders," *golot* being a Tagalog word for "mountain," and *I* a prefix meaning "people of." De Morga mentions the "Ygolotes" as owning rich mines of gold and silver, which "they work as there is need," and he goes on to say that in spite of all the diligence made to know their mines, and how they work and improve them, the matter has come to naught, "because they are cautious with the Spaniards who go to them in search of gold, and say they keep it better guarded under ground than in their houses,"

The Spaniards at a very early date sent armed exploring parties through the highlands and maintained garrisons here and there down to our own time. [2] But they never really held the country.

The Church, too, early entered this territory, the field being given over to the Dominicans, [3] who furnished many devoted missionaries to the cause. But here, too, failure must be recorded in respect of permanency of results in the really wild parts of the Highlands. It has remained for our own Government to get a real hold of the people of these regions, to win their confidence, command their respect, and exact their obedience in all relations in which obedience is proper and just.

The indispensable material condition of success was to make the mountain country accessible. Only those who have had the fortune to travel through this country can realize how difficult this endeavor has been and must continue to be, chiefly because of the great local complexity of the mountain system, but also because of the severely destructive storms of this region, with consequent torrential violence of the streams affected. But little money, too, can be, or has been, spent for the necessary road-work. In spite of the difficulties involved, however, a system of road-making has been set on foot, the labor needed being furnished by the highlanders themselves in lieu of a road tax. Very briefly, the system is as follows:

(*a*) The first thing done is to open what is known as the "meter trail," i.e., a trail one meter wide, at a grade not to exceed 6 per cent, and where possible to be kept at 4 per cent. At certain points where the absolute necessity exists, a 10 per cent grade is admissible for very short distances, as at river crossings, but only where a gentler grade would involve a long detour at great expense.

This "meter trail" weathers for one year, and thus automatically develops its own weak spots. These are repaired as fast as discovered (which is practically at once, by reason of constant supervision), and the trail thus hardens, as it were, into something approaching permanency.

(*b*) The next step in the history of the trail is to widen it to two meters, the same general course being followed as outlined in (*a*). As a satisfactory state of permanency is reached we come to (*c*) The final widening, draining, and metalling of the trail to accommodate wagon traffic. The trail now becomes a permanent road.

In many cases only wooden tools have been available, and the lack of money has compelled a sparing use of explosives. Nevertheless under this system there now exist in the Mountain Province 730 miles of excellent horse trail of easy grade, [4] and what is significant, the people of the highlands are using these trails, and so becoming peacefully acquainted with one another.

The Mountain Province itself is the outcome of the difficulties encountered in governing the wild tribes so long as these were left in provinces where either their interests were not paramount, or else the difficulties of administration were unduly costly or difficult. Established in 1908, it has a Governor, and each of its seven sub-provinces a Lieutenant-Governor, the sub-province as far as possible including people of one and of only one tribe. The creation of this province was a great step forward in promoting the welfare of the highlanders.

A word must be said here in explanation of the nomenclature of the mountain tribes. Generically, having in mind the meaning of the word, they are all Igorots. But it is the practice to distinguish the various elements of this great family by different names, restricting the term "Igorot" to special branches, as Benguet Igorot, Bontok Igorot, meaning those who live in Benguet or Bontok. The other members are known as Ifugao, Ilongot, Kalinga, and so on. [5] Lastly, the following extract from the "Census of the Philippine Islands" [6] gives some idea of the mountain system in which dwell the people whom we are about to visit.

"West of this Valley [the Cagayan] and separating it from the China Sea, stands a broad and complex system of mountains, known as the Caraballos Occidentales. Its length is nearly 200 miles, and its breadth, including the great spurs and subordinate ranges and ridges on either side, is fully one-third its length. The central range of the system forms the divide between the waters flowing to Cagayan River on the east and those flowing to the China Sea on the west. Its northern part bears the name Cordillera Norte. Farther south it is called Cordillera Central, while the southern portion is called Cordillera Sur." "At its south end the Cordillera Sur swings to the east, and, under the name of Caraballos Sur, joins the Sierra Madre, or East Coast Range."

This description, it must be understood, gives no adequate idea of the local intricacy of the system, while at the same time it is precisely this intricacy, both vertical and horizontal, that increases the cost and difficulty of making roads, and that has served in the past to keep the inhabitants of these regions apart.

CHAPTER II

Annual inspection of the mountain tribes. - We set out from Baguio. - Pangasinan Province. - Agno River. - Reception by the people.

Every year Mr. Worcester makes a formal tour of inspection through the Mountain Province to note the progress of the trails and roads, to listen to complaints, to hear reports, devise ways and means of betterment and in general to see how the hillmen are getting on. This tour is a very great affair to the highlanders, who are assembled in as great numbers as possible at the various points where stops are made; during the stay of the "Commission" (as Mr. Worcester is universally called by the highlanders) at the points of assemblage, the wild people are subsisted by the Government.

The trip is long and hard, nor is it altogether free from danger. Preparations have to be made two months ahead to have forage for animals, and food for human beings, at the expected halts, while everything eaten by man or beast on the way must be carried by the *cargadores* (bearers) who accompany the column, since living off the country is in general impossible. Under these circumstances but very few guests can be invited. I was so fortunate as to be one of these in 1910; how fortunate, I did not realize until the trip was over. For although an American may ride alone unmolested through the country we visited, still he would see only what might fall under his eye as he made his way; whereas, on this official trip, thousands of people are brought together at designated points, and one can thus do and see in a month what it would take a much longer time to do and see under one's own efforts.

This year (1910) the party was made up of Mr. Cameron Forbes, the Governor-General of the Philippine Islands; Mr. Worcester, Secretary of the Interior; Dr. Heiser, Director of Health; Dr. Strong, Chief of the Biological Laboratory; Mr. Pack, Governor of the Mountain Province; and of two officers besides myself, Captain Cootes, 13th Cavalry, Aide de Camp to the Governor-General, and Captain Van Schaick, 16th Infantry, Governor of Mindoro. General Sir Harry Broadwood, commanding His Majesty's forces at Hong Kong, had been invited, but at the last moment cabled that his duties would prevent his coming. Unless he reads this book he will never know what he missed! As we passed through the various sub-provinces their respective governors and one or two officials would join us and ride to the boundary.

On account of the difficulties of supply and transportation, we were requested to bring no *muchachos* (boys - i.e., servants), so we had to shift for ourselves. Our baggage was very strictly limited; each man being allowed two parcels, one of bedding, and the other of clothes, neither to be more than could be easily carried on the back of a single *cargador*. Mr. Worcester took along for the whole party an ingenious apparatus of his own contrivance for boiling drinking-water, as all streams in the Philippines at a level lower than 6,000 feet have been found to contain amoebae,

[7] the parasitic presence of which in the intestines produces that frightful disease, amoebic dysentery. We were especially desired to leave our revolvers at home, and had no escort.

Accordingly, our mounts and kit having been sent on a day or two in advance, we set out from Baguio in motor-cars, April 26, at eight A.M., of an extraordinarily fine day. The day before it had rained mercilessly; not only that, but clouds and mists had enveloped us so that one could not see twenty yards ahead. We were nearing the rainy season, and conditions were uncertain, but this morning the gods were on our side and we could not have asked for better weather. We went down the splendid Benguet Road, following the bed of the Bued River [8] to the railway, a drop of over 4,000 feet in thirteen miles. Strange to say, the stream had not risen at all, a fortunate circumstance, as one hundred and sixty bridges are crossed in the drop, and at times a rise will wash out not only the bridges, but all semblance of a road. [9] At the railway we turned south over the great plain of Pangasinan. This, in respect of roads, is the show province of the Archipelago and deserves its reputation, one hundred and twenty miles having been built. Those we passed over this day would have been called good in France even. Our passage was of the nature of a progress, thanks to the presence of the Governor-General. Simple bamboo arches crossing the road greeted us everywhere, Mr. Forbes punctiliously raising his hat under every one. All the villages had decorated their houses; handkerchiefs, petticoats, red table-cloths, anything and everything had been hung out of the windows by way of flags and banners. Across the front of the municipal building of one village was stretched a banner with this inscription,

"En honor de la venida del Gobernador General y de su Comitiva" ("In honor of the arrival of the Governor-General and of his retinue"), and then below on the next band, *"Deseamos iener un pozo artesiano"* ("We should like to have an Artesian well"), which led Mr. Worcester to remark that four years before the banner would have demanded *"independencia"* (independence), and not an Artesian well.

Even in Pangasinan, good roads must come to an end, and ours did as we neared the Agno River. For this blessed river is a curse to its neighborhood, and rises in flood from a stream say seventy-five yards wide to a rushing lake, if the expression be permitted, half a mile and more across. Our car finally refused to move; its wheels simply turned *in situ*, so deep was the sand. There was nothing for it but to walk to the river bank, where we were met with many apologies. A bamboo bridge had been built across the stream a few days before so that our cars might cross, but yesterday's rain had washed it down, and would we try to cross on rafts? We looked at the rafts, bamboo platforms built over large *bancas* (canoes, double-enders cut out of a single log), the bamboos being lashed together with *bejuco* (rattan, the native substitute for nails), and decided that no self-respecting motor would stand such transportation, but would go to the bottom first by overturning. So we got our stuff aboard the rafts, were poled over, and made the rest of the journey to Tayug, our first considerable halt, in *carromatas* (the native two-wheeled, springless cart). Fortunately the distance was short, the *carromata* being an instrument of torture happily overlooked by the Spanish Inquisition.

At Tayug a great concourse of people welcomed us, with arches, flags, and decorations. The *presidencia*, or town hall, was filled with the notabilities, and Mr. Forbes was presented with an address by one of the *senoritas*. Suitable answer having been made, we adjourned, the men first, the women following when we had done, according to native custom, to the side rooms, where a surprisingly good tiffin had been got ready for us, venison, chickens, French rolls, *dulces* (sweets), whiskey and soda, Heaven knows what else, to which, all unwitting of our doom, we did full justice. About two miles beyond Tayug lies San Francisco, the initial point of our real mounted journey. The people along this part of the road had simply outdone themselves in the matter of arches, there being one at every hundred yards almost. At San Francisco the crowd was greater than at Tayug; and here was set out for us another sumptuous tiffin, in a house built the day before for this very purpose, of bamboo and nipa palm. Access to it was had by a ladder and we sat down at a table, while the *senoras* of the place waited on us, every inch of standing-room being occupied by people who had crowded in to see the performance of the Governor-General and of his *comitiva!* And perform we did - we had to! Ducks, chickens, venison, *camotes* (sweet potatoes), peppers, beer, red wine - no one would have thought that but three-quarters of an hour before we had just gone through the same thing. But it would have been the height of discourtesy to give way to our inclination by showing a lack of appetite; moreover, it is not often that a party is held in a house built to be used merely one hour. So we did honor to the occasion, but had to let out our belts before mounting immediately afterward.

CHAPTER III

Padre Juan Villaverde. - His great trail. - The beginning of the mountain journey. - Nozo.

The point to which we had come, San Francisco, marks the beginning of the Juan Villaverde trail from the Central Valley of Luzon through the mountains before us, to the province of Nueva Vizcaya. All day the chain we were to pierce had been in sight, and I for one had been wondering where we were to find a practicable entrance, so forbiddingly vertical did the range appear to be.

Now the Spaniards in the Philippines at best were but poor road-or trail-makers. Indeed, in the matter of trails they were simply stupid, in some cases actually going straight up a hill and down the other side, when the way around was no longer, and of course far easier to maintain. But Padre Juan Villaverde of the Dominicans was a great and honorable exception. Quite apart from this aspect, we hear so much that is evil of the friars that it is a pleasure, when possible, to point out the good they did, a thing more frequently possible than people imagine it is. For Father Villaverde gave his life to missionary work among the hill-people, seeking in every way to better their condition materially as well as morally. Born in 1841, as early as 1868 we find him on duty at Bayombong, in Nueva Vizcaya, the province we were about to enter.

From the first he seems to have been impressed by the possibilities of the country in which he was laboring; and, foreseeing that good communications would ultimately settle most of the questions relating to the highlanders, he built trails, trails that are still in use, whereas nearly all the others (but few in number) established by the Spaniards have been abandoned by us, where Nature has not indeed saved us the trouble by washing them out of existence. For thirty years Villaverde worked unceasingly, building roads and bridges and churches, and striving to civilize the people among whom he lived; but his chief work, that by which his memory is kept green to this day, is the great trail from the otherwise almost inaccessible province of Nueva Vizcaya, across the Caraballos to the Central Valley of Luzon, where access to the outer world by rail becomes possible. This trail is officially designated by his name, and is maintained by Government. This was the one we were about to enter upon. [10] Accordingly we thanked our kind hosts of San Francisco; and at last set out on our real trip. But, curious and eager as I felt to engage upon it, I could not help regretting that this part of our journey was over, that we had to turn our backs on the smiling plains of Pangasinan, its hospitable and courteous people. The day had been so cool and fresh, and our progress so easy; flat as was the country, it had its charm, the charm of cultivated plains, relieved by lanes of feathered bamboos, by clumps of nodding palms, by limpid streams. But we were off, nevertheless, the Governor-General on a cow-pony, nearly all the rest on Arabs and thoroughbreds, Van Schaick and I riding mountain ponies. We had fifteen miles to go to reach our first resting-place.

Crossing a stream, we began to climb at once, and as

we rose the plain of Central Luzon began to unroll itself below us, with our road of the morning stretching out in a straight white line through the green rice-fields. Far to the west we now and then caught glimpses of Lingayen Gulf, with the Zambales Mountains in full view running south and bordering the plain, while still farther to the south Mount Arayat [11] rose abruptly from its surrounding levels. Now Arayat is plainly visible from Manila. Here and there solitary rocky hills, looking for all the world like ant-heaps, but in reality hundreds of feet high, broke the uniformity of the plains. Flooded as the whole landscape was with brilliant sunshine, the view was exquisite in respect both of form and of color. But as we moved on, turning and twisting and ever rising, we were soon confined to just the few yards the sinuosities of the trail would allow us to see at one time. For a part of the way the country was rocky, hills bare and fire-swept; not a tree or shrub suggested that we were in the tropics. Soon pines began to appear, and then thickened, till the trail led through a pine forest, pure and simple, the ground covered with green grass, and the whole fresh and moist from recent rains. It was up and down and around and around. Not a sign of animal life did we see, not a trace of human beings.

I was disgusted, and still more disconcerted, this afternoon, to find my pony going badly. He was perfectly willing to walk, but at a most dignified rate, selected by himself. He apparently had no objection to catching up the party every now and then, but only to relapse into his funeral walk, after contact had been re-established. But then Cootes took the lead that after-noon, and as his thoroughbred had had two days' rest, and breasted all the rises with apparent joyousness, nobody was able to keep up, until Mr. Worcester took the head with his black, a powerful but reasonable animal. However, everybody gets into camp sooner or later, and so did we all at a resting-point called Nozo, where we all turned in after supper, for reveille was to be at three o'clock. This had been a great day of contrasts in a descending scale, from motors, electric lights, and telephones in the morning to our solitary camp in the mountains at night, surrounded by watch-fires and guarded by Constabulary sentinels. This, by the way, was the only time we were so guarded.

CHAPTER IV

Early start. - Pine forest. - Vegetation. - Rest at Amugan. - The *gansa*. - Bone.

We set out next morning at five-thirty. Our journey so far, that is, since we mounted, had taken us over a preliminary range, and now we began a more serious climb. The morning was delightfully fresh and cool, with promise of a fine blazing sun later. Far ahead and above us on the skyline, we could see a cut in the forest where our trail crossed the divide. But that was miles away, and in the meantime we were ascending a lovely valley, pines, grass, and bright red soil. It was delicious that morning, riding under the pines.

> "Pinea brachia cum trepidant,
> Audio canticulum zephyri!"

And part of the pleasure was due to the fact that we had an unobstructed view in all directions, usually not the case in the tropical forest. At one point we had a full view of Arayat, at another of Santo Tomas, near which we had passed yesterday on coming down from Baguio. But fine as were the distant views we got from time to time, the great attraction was the country itself, through which we were passing. Barring the total absence of any sign of man, it might have been taken for Japan, in the neighborhood of Miyanoshita, without, however, any trace of Japanese atmosphere.

The valley was steep-walled, narrow and twisting, at one point closed by a single enormous rock nearly three hundred feet high - in fact, a conical hill rising right out of the floor of the valley, and apparently leaving just room for the stream to pass on one side.

A curious fact was that while the mountains were decidedly northern-looking as to flora, yet the groins, wherever possible, were thoroughly tropical. For in these water runs off but slowly, with consequent richness of vegetation. And yet, on the other side of the divide which we were now approaching not a pine could be seen, but, on the contrary, the typical tropical forest in full development. The watershed, our skyline, was an almost absolute dividing-mark. At any rate, there the pines stopped short.

At the divide we crossed from Pangasinan into Nueva Vizcaya. And with the crossing began the forest just mentioned, and a long descent for us. Our immediate destination was Amugan, our first rest halt. It is of absolutely no use to try to describe this part of the trip. If the confusion of trees, vines, orchids, tree ferns, foliage plants, creepers, was bewildering, so was the impression produced. But we saw many examples of the most beautiful begonia in existence, in full blossom, gorgeous spheres of dark scarlet hanging above and around us. According to Mr. Worcester, all attempts to transplant it have failed. Its blossoms would be sometimes twenty and thirty feet in the air. Nothing could exceed the glory of these masses of flowers, sometimes a foot and more in diameter, as projected by the rays of the early morning sun against

Cornelis De Witt Willcox

the dark green background, the whole glistening and dripping in the rain-like dew. Tree ferns abounded; we passed one that must have been over sixty feet high. At one halt the ground about was aflame with yellow orchids, growing out of the ground. And there was one plant that I recognized myself, unaided, the wild tomato, a little thing of eight or nine inches, but holding up its head with all the rest of them. As always, on this trip, however, it was the splendor of the country that held the attention, the wild incoherent mountain masses thrown together apparently without order or system, buttressed peaks, mighty flanks riven to the core by deep valleys, radiating spurs, re-entrant gorges, the limit of vision filled by crenellated ranges in all the serenity of their distant majesty. And then, as our trail wound in and out, different aspects of the same elements would present themselves, until really the faculty of admiration became exhausted. And so on down we went, to be greeted as we neared Amugan by a sound of tom-toms; it was a party that had come out to welcome us, carrying the American flag and beating the *gansa* (tom-tom) by way of music. The *gansa*, made of bronze, in shape resembles a circular pan about twelve or thirteen inches in diameter, with a border of about two inches turned up at right angles to the face. On the march it is hung from a string and beaten with a stick. At a halt it is beaten with the open hand.

After crossing a coffee plantation, we reached a little settlement, where we off-saddled and took a bite after six hours' riding. The half-dozen houses of this tiny village are of the usual Filipino type, and the very few inhabitants were dressed after the fashion of the Christianized provinces. Nevertheless, we here first encountered the savage we had come up to see; for not only did they have the *gansa*, but they offered us a *canao*. This is a feast of which we shall have splendid examples later on, with dancing, beating of *gansas*, drinking and so on, and the sacrifice of a pig.

Here the affair was to be much smaller, all the elements being absent except the pig and drums. We had noticed as we dismounted a pig tied to a post and evidently in a very uneasy frame of mind, and justly, for, although the honor of a *canao* was declined, on account of the length of the ceremony and of the distance we had yet to go, still they were resolved upon the death of the pig. He, however, at the same time had made up his mind to escape, and by a mighty effort broke his tether, and got off; but in vain, for after a short but exciting chase he was caught and then, an incision having been made in his belly, a sharpened stick was inserted and stirred about until his insides were thoroughly mixed, when he died. We left them cleaning and scraping and dividing, and beating two drums, about four feet long, eight inches in diameter, covered with leather at one end. These are beaten with the open hand, the performer sitting on the ground with the instrument coming up over his left thigh, and produce a muffled and melancholy note. Mr. Forbes had some notion of buying one of them, but was told he would be simply wasting his time, both *gansas* and drums having an extraordinary value in the eye of their owners.

We moved on, gradually descending, rested at Santa Fe, a rest-house and nothing else, for two or three hours, and then turned north, following an affluent of the Magat River, by an old and poor trail, the new one having been washed out for three hundred yards some two or three miles ahead. And after dark we made Bone, our resting-place for the night.

CHAPTER V

Aritao. - *Bubud*. - Dupax. - Start for Campote.

We all slept in the school-house, for Bone is a Christianized village, and next day, April 28th, made a late start, for it was to be a day of easy stages. By nine oclock, passing through an undulating champaign country, we reached Aritao, being met at the outskirts by *gansa*-beaters and also by the Christian school-children with medieval-looking banners, and all in their best bibs and tuckers; the heathen and the Christians mingling apparently on the best of terms. Aritao is an old town, now much decayed, but showing evidences of former affluence. It has a brick church, the bells of which were rung on our approach.

As there is some Government here, of course we had to pay a visit of ceremony, and were accordingly received by the *presidente* and other dignitaries in an upper chamber, the little children with their banners massing around the gate of the house and forming a really pretty picture. When we were all in, the *presidente* made the Governor-General and his suite a dignified speech of welcome, very well done, to which Mr. Forbes made answer in fluent and pretty good Spanish.

Bubud was then passed about - but this is going too fast! *Bubud* (called *tapuy* elsewhere) is an institution in the parts where we now were, and I had been hearing

Cornelis De Witt Willcox

of it for days. It is the native (Ifugao) name of a drink produced by the fermentation of rice, a drink that varies in color and in flavor, according to the care taken in its make, but nearly always agreeable to the palate and refreshing. That offered us to-day was greenish yellow, slightly acid and somewhat bitter from the herbs added. Unfortunately, it will not bear transportation, but we made up for this by carrying off personally as much as was convenient. It had a happy effect on my pony, too: all the way to Aritao he had been slower than the wrath to come, but from this on he showed life and spirit; in fact, he danced and pranced through every town we crossed for some days afterward. I always meant to ask if some one had given him any *bubud* at Aritao, during the speech-making; on reflection I am inclined to doubt it, but at any rate, in honor of the circumstances, he was known as Bubud the rest of the trip.

A short ride through the charming, smiling country (part of it might have been France), over a really good road most of the way, brought us to Dupax. On the way we were met by some of the American officials of the province, among them Mr. Norman Connor, Superintendent of Education (Yale, 1900), and by two Belgian priests, De Wit of Dupax and Van der Maes of Bayombong. The natives met us, all mounted, with a band, so that we made a triumphant entrance, advancing in line to the *presidente's* house, while the church-bell pealed out a welcome.

Dupax must, like Aritao, have been a point of some importance in the past. It has a large brick church with a decidedly Flemish facade, and a detached pagoda-like belfry. Its streets are overgrown with fine soft grass, and its houses had somehow or other an air of comfort and ease. Here we made quite a stop, first of all quenching our thirst with *bubud*, beer, cocoanut milk, anything, everything, for we had ridden nearly all the way so far in the sun. We then sat down to an excellent breakfast, and smoked and lounged about until two, when fresh ponies were brought, and we set off on a side trip to Campote, where we were to have our first contact with the real wild man, the Ilongot. [12]

CHAPTER VI

The Ilongots and their country. - Efforts of our Government to reach these people. - The forest trail. - Our first contact with the wild man.

These people, the Ilongots, although very few in number, only six thousand, stretch from Nueva Vizcaya to the Pacific Coast, inhabiting an immense region of forested and all but inaccessible mountains. Over these they roam without any specially fixed habitation. They have the reputation, and apparently deserve it, of being cruel and treacherous, as they certainly are shy and wild. It was these people who killed Doctor Jones, of the Marshall Field Museum, after he had been with them eight or nine months. So recently as 1907 they made a descent on Dupax, killing people and taking their heads. When they mean to kill a man fairly, according to their ideas, they hand him a fish. This is a signal that he must be on his guard: to refuse the fish is of no use, because by so doing one puts one's self beyond the pale, and may be killed in any fashion. We heard a story here of a Negrito stealing a pig from two Ilongots who had a Negrito brother-in-law. Failing to recover the pig, they decided that they must have a Negrito head, and so took their brother-in-law's. Pig-stealing, by the way, in the mountain country is regarded much as horse-stealing used to be out West. Besides the spear and head knife, the Ilongots, like the Negritos, with whom they have intermarried to a certain extent, use the bow and arrow, and are correspondingly dreaded. For it seems to be believed in Luzon that bow-and-arrow savages are more dangerous than spear-and-ax-men; that the use of this projectile weapon, the arrow, induces craftiness, hard to contend against. An Ilongot can silently shoot you in the back, after you have passed. A spear-man has to get closer, and can not use an ambush so readily. [13]

Now our Government in the Philippines, by and through and because of Mr. Worcester, had made repeated efforts to reach these Ilongots, to bring them in, as it were, and only recently had these efforts met with any success. For one thing, it is a very serious matter to seek them out in the depths of their fastnesses if only because of the difficulty of reaching them; many of them even now have never seen a white man, and would escape, if I recollect aright, on the approach of our people. But in 1908 some fifty of them did "come in," and, gaining confidence, this number grew to one hundred and fifty in 1909. They, or some of them at least, now sent an invitation to Mr. Worcester to come and see them, and he accepted on condition of their making a trail, saying that they could not expect a man of his stature to creep through their country on his hands and knees. This trail they had built, and they had assembled at Campote, four hours from Dupax, for this first formal visit; It was the desire of Mr. Worcester that this visit should be happy in all respects; for, if not, the difficulties of intercourse with this people, already great, would be so seriously increased as to delay the civilizing intentions of the Government for many years to come.

We rode off at about two o'clock , passing under

numberless bamboo arches, on an astonishingly good road, built by Padre Juan Villaverde. About two miles out we left the road, turning off east across rice-paddies, and then followed a stream, which we crossed near the foot of a large bare mountain facing south. Up this we zigzagged four miles, a tiresome stretch with the sun shining full upon us. But at the top we had our reward: to the south reached a beautiful open valley, its floor a mass of green undulations, its walls purple mountains blazing in the full glory of the afternoon sun. At the extreme south, miles away, we could make out Las Salinas, Salt Springs, [14] whose deposits sparkled and shone and scintillated and danced in the heated air. Grateful as it would have been to rest at the top and enjoy the scene, we nevertheless had to turn our backs upon it, for we had yet far to go over an unknown trail, and it was most desirable to get in before dark. So we turned and now plunged into a forest of tall trees so thick overhead and so deeply buried in vines, and creepers and underbrush generally, that just as no light got in from above, so one could not see ten yards in any direction off the trail. This effect was no doubt partly due to the shades of evening, and to our being on the eastern slope of the mountain. And that trail! The Ilongots, poor chaps, had done their best with it, and the labor of construction must have been fearful. [15] But the footing was nothing but volcanic mud, laterite, all the worse from a recent rain. Our ponies sank over their fetlocks at every step, and required constant urging to move at all. Compared to the one I was riding, Bubud was a race-horse! Cootes, Strong, and I kept together, the others having ridden on. As the day grew darker and darker, the myriad notes of countless insects melted into one mighty, continuous shrill note high overhead, before us, behind us, in which not one break or intermission could be detected. Anything faster than a walk would now have been unsafe, even if it had been possible, for at times the ground sloped off sharply down the mountain, the footing grew more and more uncertain, and part of the time we could not see the trail at all. Indeed, Cootes's pony stepped in a hole and fell, pitching Cootes clean over his head, and sending his helmet down the mountain-side, where Cootes had to go and get it. Soon after this, though, the forest thinned perceptibly, the trail grew better, and we met Connor, who had turned back to see how we were getting on, and who informed us we had only one-half hour more before us. Going on, we were greeted by a shout of welcome from our first Ilongot, standing in the trail, subligate, or gee-stringed, otherwise stark naked, and armed with a spear, the sentinel of a sort of outpost, equally naked, with which we soon came up. They were all armed, too, spears and shields, and all insisted on shaking hands with every one of us. You must shake hands when they offer to, an unpleasant matter sometimes, when you notice that the man who is paying you this attention is covered with *toenia imbricata*, or other rare tropical skin disease. [16] *Noblesse oblige*, here as elsewhere; besides, a consideration for your own skin may require you to put aside your prejudices. The trail now turned down over a broad, cleared hog-back, at the flattened end of which we could see two shacks and a temporary shed for our mounts. Smoke was rising cheerfully in the air and people were moving about. This was Campote.

CHAPTER VII

School at Campote. - Our white pony, and the offer made for his tail.

It was too dark by this time to see or do much. We had supper, looked up the place where we were to sleep, and then collected at the lower of the two shacks. Here we received visits, so to say, from as many Ilongots, grown men only, as could get into the place. In truth, we were as much objects of curiosity to them as they possibly could have been to us. To Mr. Worcester the occasion was one of business, explaining through interpreters why we had come, what the Government wanted, getting acquainted with the *cabecillas* (head men), and listening to what they had themselves to say. One of our visitors was a grandfather, remarkable, first, because of his heavy long beard, and, second, because his own grandfather was alive; five generations of one family in existence at the same time.

Campote, I may as well say it here as anywhere else, is merely a point where Connor has established a school for children, under a Christianized Filipino teacher. Some thirty children in all are under instruction, the average attendance being twenty-four. It is almost impossible, so Connor told us, to make these people understand why children should go to school, or what a school is, or is for, anyway. However, a beginning has been made. They all have a dose of "the three Rs"; the boys are taught, besides, carpentry, gardening, and rope-making, and the girls sewing, weaving, and thread-making from cotton grown by the boys on the spot. They ought to show some skill in all these arts; for the native rice-basket is a handsome, strong affair, square of cross-section, with sides flaring out, and about three feet high, and some of their weapons show great manual skill. The garden was on show the next morning, displaying beans, tomatoes, cotton, perhaps other things that I failed to recognize or have forgotten, anyway, a sufficient garden. There is besides an exchange here for the sale of native wares.

One of our party had ridden a white pony, and was much amused, as were all of us, to receive an offer for his tail! There is nothing else the Ilongots hold in higher estimation than white horse-hair, and here was a pony with a tail full of it! But the offer was refused; the idea of cutting off the tail was not to be entertained for one moment. Certainly, he might keep its tail: what they wanted was the hair. Would he sell the hair? No; that was only a little less bad than to sell the tail itself.

On our way back to the shack in which some of us were to sleep (the school-house it was) we noticed an admiring crowd standing around the pony, tethered under the house, and all unconscious of the admiration he was exciting, most rudely presenting his hind-quarters to his admirers. But that was not his intention; the crowd - half women, by the way - wanted to be as close to the tail as possible. We left them gesticulating and pointing and commenting, much as our own women might while looking at crown jewels, but not so hopelessly; for the next morning, when we next saw the pony, nearly all the hair had been pulled out of his tail, except a few patches or tufts here or there, tougher than the rest, and serving now merely to show what the original dimensions must have been.

While we were undressing in came a little maiden, who marched up to every one of us, shook hands, and said, "Good evening, sir." We were pretty well undressed, but our lack of clothes looked perfectly natural to her, perhaps inspired her with confidence. She said her name was Banda, that she was thirteen, but of this she could not know, as all these children had had ages assigned to them when they entered the school; after greeting us all, and airing her slight stock of English, she withdrew as properly as she had entered. A trifling incident, perhaps not worth recording, but in reality significant, for it marked confidence, especially as she had come in of her own accord. We all agreed that she was very pretty.

CHAPTER VIII

Appearance of the Ilongots. - Dress. - Issue of beads and cloth. - Warrior dance. - School work. - Absence of old women from meeting.

The next morning we turned out early, and got our first real "look-see." Campote is completely surrounded by mountains, the hogback dropping off into the valley below us. About four or five hundred people had assembled, men, women, and children. As a rule, they were small and well built, but not so well built as the tribes farther north. The men were fully armed with spears, bows and arrows, shields, and head-knives; gee-strings apart, they were naked. Some of them wore on the head the scarlet beak of the hornbill; these had taken heads. Quite a number, both men and women, had a small cross-like pattern tattooed on the forehead; the significance of this I did not learn. The shield is in one piece, in longitudinal cross-section like a very wide flat V open toward the bearer, the top terminating in a piece rising between two scoops, one on each side of the median line. The women had on short skirts and little jackets (like what, I am told, we call bolero jackets), the bosom being bare. Around the waist they wore bands of brass wire or of bamboo stained red and wound around with fine brass wire. These bamboo bands were pretty and artistic. You saw the children as they happened to be; the only thing to note about them being that they were quite bright-looking. What the

Cornelis De Witt Willcox

men lacked in clothes they made up in their hair, for they wore it long and some of them had it done up in the most absolute Psyche knots. Such earrings as we saw were worn in the upper cartilage of the ear. It may be remarked, too, that the women had a contented and satisfied air, as though sure of their power and position; we found this to be the case generally throughout the Mountain Country.

The purpose of the visit being to cultivate pleasant relations with and receive the confidence of these shy people, the real business of the day was soon opened. Mr. Worcester took his place in the shade of his shack, and proceeded to the distribution of red calico, beads, combs, mirrors, and other small stuff, the people coming up by *rancherias* (settlements or villages); none of the highlanders seem to have any conception of tribal organization, a condition no doubt due to the absence of communications. A *cabecilla*, or head man, would receive two meters, his wife one, and others smaller measures. This sort of thing was carefully studied out, so far as rank was concerned, for it would never do to give a common person even approximately as much as a *cabecilla*. One *rancheria* would take all red beads, another white, another blue, and so on. Not once did I see a trace of greediness or even eagerness, though interest was marked. The whole thing was conducted in the most orderly fashion, the various *rancherias* awaiting their turn with exemplary patience. [17]

The issue over, dancing began. In this only men and boys took part, to the music of small rude fiddles, tuned in fifths, [18] played by the men, and of a queer instrument consisting of two or three joints of bamboo with strings stretched over bridges, beaten with little sticks by the women. The fiddles must be of European origin. The orchestra, seven or eight all told, sat in the shade, surrounded by an admiring crowd. Among them was a damsel holding a civilized umbrella over her head, whereof the stick and the rib-points were coquettishly decorated with white horse-hair tied in little brushes, doubtless furnished by our white pony.

The dancing at once fixed our attention. Two or three men, though usually only two, took position on the little terreplein below the shack, and began a slow movement, taking very short, formal, staccato steps in a circle against the sun. Keeping back to back and side to side, they maintained the whole body in a tense, rigid posture with the chest out, head up and thrown back, abdomen drawn in, right hand straight out, the left also, holding a shield, eyes glazed and fixed, knees bent forward. Between the steps, the dancers would stand in this strained, tense position, then move forward a few inches, and so on around the circle. After a little of this business, for that is just what it was, the next part came on, a simulation of fighting: and, as everything before was as stiff, strained, and rigid as it was possible to be, so now everything was light, graceful, agile, and quick; leaps forward and back, leaps sideways, the two combatants maneuvering, as it were, one around the other, for position. It was hard to realize that human motions could be so graceful, light and easy. Then head-knives were drawn, and cuts right, and cuts left, cuts at every part of the body from the head to the ankles, were added to the motion; the man on the defensive for the moment making suitable parries with his shield.

The dance completed, the dancers would advance and face Mr. Worcester, put their heels together in true military fashion, hold their arms out right and left, and make a slight inclination of the head, a sort of salute, in fact, to the one they regarded as the principal personage of the party.

We saw much dancing later on in our trip, but none that equalled this in intensity and character, apart from its being of a totally different kind, Heiser managed, with some difficulty, to take a photograph of the tense phase of one of the dances; it gives a better idea of the phase than my imperfect description.

The dancing was followed by archery, the target being a small banana stem at some thirty paces. This calls for no especial comment, except that many hits were made, and many of the misses would have hit a man. More interesting was an ambush they laid for us, to show how they attacked. While collecting for it, to our astonishment the entire party suddenly ran in all directions at top speed and hid behind whatever offered. On their return, in four or five minutes, they explained that a spirit had suddenly appeared among them, and that they had had to run. On our asking how they knew a spirit had turned up, they asked if we had not noticed leaves and grass flying in a spiral. As a matter of fact, some of us had, a very small and very gentle whirlwind having formed for a second or two. They had seen it, too, and that was the spirit.

It was now mid-day; we had *tiffin*, and began preparations for our departure. The various arms, shields, and other things we had bought were collected to be cargadoed back to Pangasinan. Among them, alas! were not two beautiful head-knives, which their wearers had absolutely declined to part with on any terms whatever. They resisted the Governor-General even. I give a photograph here of a knife and scabbard that Connor sent me on later. It is a handsome one, but not as handsome as those two jewels!

Our last performance was to look at the garden and to see the school at work, making thread and rope, weaving mats, and so on. I take it that this school was really the significant thing at Campote, apart from the significance of the occasion itself. We spent but little time over it, however, our interest in the arts of war having left us only a few minutes for those of peace. Nevertheless, here is a beginning that will bear fruit, and in the meantime Connor rides alone and in safety among these wild people, which proves a good many things, when you select the right man to do your hard work.

Mr. Worcester, as we rode off, expressed the liveliest satisfaction with the meeting. These people, returning to their *rancherias*, he said, would talk for a year of their treatment at the hands of the Americans, of the gift of *palay* (rice) to four hundred people, for two days, to say nothing of two *vacas* (cows) and of other gifts. Next year, he hoped, half of them would come in; besides, the start made was good; the presence of so many women and children was a good sign, and equally good was the total absence of old women. For these are a source of trouble and mischief with their complaints of the degeneracy of the times. They address themselves particularly to the young men, accusing them of a lack of courage and of other parts, taunting them with the fact that the young women will have none of them, that in *their* day *their* young men brought in heads, etc. Thus it has happened, especially when any native drink was going about, that trouble has followed. It is the practice, therefore, of our

Cornelis De Witt Willcox

Government when arranging these meetings to suggest that the old women be left at home, and if so left, it is a good indication.

CHAPTER IX

Return to civilization. - Reception at Bambang. -
Aglipayanos and Protestants.

The return to the main road from Campote was a great
improvement over the advance. The sun had partly
dried the trail, and his vertical rays enabled us to see
about us a little, and realize what a tremendous pheno-
menon tropical vegetation can be. Some Philippine
trees, for example, the *narra*, throw out buttresses. One
we saw on this trail must have measured twenty feet
across on the ground, from vertex to vertex of
diametrically opposite buttresses, the bole itself not
being over two and one-half feet in diameter, and the
buttresses starting about fifteen feet above the ground.
But the greatest difference to me personally was in my
mount, Connor having lent me his pony, as admirable
as mine of the day before had been wretched. In spite
of the fact that Connor had to stay behind at Campote
and could catch us up later, this attention on his part
was one of the most generous things that ever
happened to me, for certainly the pony he got from me
was the most irritating piece of horseflesh imaginable.
I am glad publicly to give him my warmest thanks
again! Mr. Worcester was well mounted, too; he rode
this day at two hundred and thirty-five pounds, and his
kit must have weighed some thirty more, yet his little
beast carried him soundly to Bambang, our destination,
about seventeen miles, twelve of them at a "square,

unequivocal" trot, by no means an unusual example of the strength and endurance of some of these native ponies. In what seemed a very short time (but the trail was comparatively dry) we broke out of the forest, and again had our lovely valley below and in front of us. At the top we saw some giant fly-catchers, a bird of so powerful and erratic a flight that no one has so far, according to Mr. Worcester, succeeded in killing one of them. It may be mentioned here that we saw very few birds or any other animals on our journey. Shortly after beginning the descent, some of the party, impatient of the zig-zags, decided to go straight down, the temptation being a cool green stream at the foot of the mountain; half an hour afterward, on turning a point, we could see them disporting themselves in the waters, and at that distance looking very much like Diana and her nymphs in the usual pictures.

Back in the main road, we stopped to rest at a point covered with a sensitive plant so delicate that, on stepping on it anywhere, the nervous thrill, if that is what it is, would run three or four feet or more in all directions before dying down. From this point we turned north, our way taking us through a broad open valley, past rice-fields and between clumps of flowering guava bushes. As we neared Bambang, where we were to spend the night, we were as before met by the local notabilities on horseback; and breasting a rise, we saw our road down in the plain in which this town lies, lined on both sides by all the school-children of the place, dressed in their very best clothes, some of them American fashion with shoes and stockings and looking mighty uncomfortable in consequence. Nearly everyone had a flag. Riding into the town, we found the *plaza* crowded with men and women, dressed mostly in white, and what with the flags, the church-bells clanging with all their might, the crowd, and the children trooping in, our cavalcade made a triumphant entrance.

We dismounted at the *presidente's*, where muscatel and cocoanut milk were given us. A little muscatel goes a long way, but this is not true of the milk when one's tongue is hanging out from riding in the sun, and there are only two or three cocoanuts. Filipinos apparently are not fond of this drink, and we nearly always had to send out and get more. No sooner were we in the house than addresses began, one of these being in Ilokano. The native language of Bambang, however, is the Isanay, spoken elsewhere only at Aritao and Dupax, a dying tongue, doomed to early extinction.

Bambang, like nearly all the other Nueva Vizcaya towns we had seen or were to see, shows signs of decadence. It has a good church and *convento*, a great *plaza*, and is surrounded by a fertile country, but something is missing. After dinner, I went over and called on the padre, one of the Belgians, whom we had met the day before. He informed me that Bambang had many Protestants, which he explained by the sharp rivalry between the *Aglipayanos*, or members of the "native" church, headed by the secessionist Aglipay, and the Catholics. To avoid the issues raised by this rivalry, many natives would appear to have abandoned the errors of Rome (or of *Aglipayanismo*, as the case may be) for those of the Reformation.

When I got back to the *presidente's*, everybody had turned in, and the house was dark. However, I found a bed not occupied by anyone else, but of my bedding there was not a sign. So I stretched out on the *petate*

Cornelis De Witt Willcox

[19] of my bed, only to wake up later shivering with cold, which I tried to remedy by fishing around for cover in a pile of straw mats, from which I extracted what turned out in the morning to be a *jusi* table-cloth, through which you could have shot straws. It is altogether a mistake to imagine that one can not be cold in the tropics.

CHAPTER X

Magat River. - Enthusiastic reception at Bayombong. - Speeches and reports. - Solano. - Ifugao " college yell." - Bagabag.

The next day, April 20, we rode out at six, a splendid morning; Bubud felt the inspiration, too, for he got on capitally. We soon reached the Magat River on the other side of which was Bayombong, the capital of the province and our first halt of the day.

The Magat is another of those turbulent, uncertain rivers of the Archipelago; we were not sure as we neared it whether we could get over or not. When up, it carries waves in midstream six to seven feet from crest to trough. But we had no such ill-luck, and *bancas* soon came over for us, the horses swimming. While waiting for them we had a chance to admire the beautiful country; on one side tall spreading trees and broad savannahs, on the other the mountain presenting a bare scarp of red rock many hundreds of feet high; immediately in front the cool, green river, over all the brilliant sun, not yet too hot to prevent our thinking of other things.

Once over, we had no occasion to complain of our reception! All the notabilities were present, of course, mounted, but in addition there were three bands, all playing different tunes at the same time, in different

Cornelis De Witt Willcox

keys, and all *fortissimo*. No instrument was allowed to rest, the drums being especially vigorous. One of the bands was that of the Constabulary, playing really well, and with magnificent indifference to the other two. I am bound to say they returned it. We had the Constabulary troops, too, as escort, a well set-up, well-turned-out and soldierlike body. What with the bands, the pigs, the dogs, the horses, the children, the people, it was altogether one of the most delightful confusions conceivable, not the least interesting feature being the happy unconsciousness of the people of the incongruity of the reception. However, we formed a column, the Constabulary at the head, with its band, and were played into Bayombong, with the other bands, children, dogs, etc., as a mighty rear guard.

Our first business was to listen to reports and addresses. So we all went upstairs in the Government House, the *presidencia*; the Governor-General, Mr. Worcester, and the *presidente* took their seats on a dais, while the rest of us, with the local Americans and some of the native inhabitants, formed the audience, and listened to a report read by the treasurer. This made a great impression on us, so sensible and businesslike was it; not content with a statement, it went on to describe the affairs of the province, the possibilities of agriculture, and what could be accomplished if the people would turn to and work, and in particular it made no complaints. Apparently this report alarmed the *presidente*, for he left his seat on the platform as soon as he decently could, and delivered a speech intended to traverse the treasurer's report. His concern was almost comic: the idea of saying to the Governor-General that a great deal could be done locally by work, when there was a central Government at Manila! Mr. Forbes, as usual, made in his turn a very sound speech, based on his observation in the province, on its fertility, its possibilities, the necessity of improving communications and of diversifying crops. I noticed here, as elsewhere in the province, the excellence of the Spanish used in speeches. As for the treasurer, we were informed that he had been taken in hand at an early age by the Americans and trained, so that in making his reports he had developed the ability to look upon the merits of the question in hand. But he must feel himself to be a unique person!

We rested here in Bayombong through the heat of the day, part going to Governor Bryant's house, the rest of us to that of Captain Browne, the local Inspector of Constabulary. I have a grateful recollection of his hospitality, as well as of that of his brother officers, with whom we dined. Nor must I forget the Standard Oil Company. For had not Browne rigged up a shower, consisting of the Standard five-gallon tin? A *muchacho* filled it with water and pulled it up over a pulley, and you got an excellent shower from the holes punched in the bottom. In fact, the Standard five-gallon tin is as well known in the East as its contents, and is carefully preserved and used. We had several opportunities to bless its existence.

Pleasant as was the nooning, it had to end: we mounted and rode on to Solano. On the way Bubud insisted on drinking from a dirty swamp by the roadside, although there was a limpid stream not fifty yards ahead which he could see as well as I. But there was nothing for it but the swamp; I accordingly let him have his way, only to find the bank slippery and the water deep, so that he went in up to his shoulders, with his hindquarters on the bank. While I was trying to pull him back, he got in his hindquarters, and then, in further answer to my efforts, sat down in the water! And such water! Thick, greasy, smelly! A *carabao* wallow it was. He now gave unmistakable evidence of an intention to lie down, when a friendly hand got me up on the bank, whereupon Bubud, concluding he would get out too, emerged with a coat of muddy slime. This seemed to have no effect whatever on his spirits, for on entering Solano a few minutes later, to the sound of bells and bands, with banners fluttering in the breeze, he got into such a swivet that before I knew it he was at the head of the procession, having worked himself forward and planted himself squarely in front of the Governor-General's horse, where he caracoled and curvetted and pranced to his heart's delight. As soon as we got out of the *barrio*, he was quite satisfied to take a more modest position, but occasions of ceremony seemed to deprive him of all realization of his proper place in the world.

The people of Solano made a great effort to have us stay the night, but it was impossible; we had to get on to Bagabag. Solano, by the way, is the commercial emporium of this end of the province, for there is not a single shop in Bayombong. So on we went, through a calm, dignified afternoon, the country as before impressing me with its open, smiling valleys, its broad fields, its air of expectant fertility, inviting one to come scratch its surface, if no more, in order to reap abundant harvests. In fact, it seemed to me that we were riding through typical farming land at home, instead of through a Malay valley under the tropic. And if anything more were needed to strengthen the illusion, it was a college yell, given by a gang of Ifugaos (the people we were now immediately on our way to visit) repairing a bridge we had to cross! They did it in style, and naturally had no cheer-leader; time was kept by beating on the floor of the bridge with tools. For this uttering of a shout of welcome or of other emotion in unison is a characteristic trait of the Ifugaos, like their using spoons, and can be likened to nothing else in the world but our American college yell.

Our reception at Bagabag was much like all the others we had had: bands, arches, addresses, one in excellent English. But on this occasion, after listening to a speech telling how poor the people were, how bad the roads were, how much they needed Government help, etc., etc., Mr. Forbes squared off in his answer, and told them a few things, as that he had seen so far not a single lean, hungry-looking person, that the elements were kindly, that they could mend their own roads, and that he was tired of their everlasting complaint of poverty and hunger, when a little work would go a great way in this country toward bettering their material condition. This, of course, is just the kind of talk these people need, and the last some of them wish to hear.

CHAPTER XI

We enter the Mountain Province.-Payawan. - Kiangan, its position. - Anitos. - Speech of welcome by Ifugao chief. - Detachment of native Constabulary. - Visit of Ifugao chiefs to our quarters. - Dancing.

We were now on the borders of the Mountain Province; literally one more river to cross, and we should turn our backs on Nueva Vizcava. And with regret, for it is a beautiful smiling province, of fertile soil, of polite and hospitable people, of lovely mountains, limpid streams and triumphant forests. In Dampier's quaint words, spoken of another province, but equally true of this one, "The Valleys are well moistened with pleasant Brooks, and small Rivers of delicate Water; and have Trees of divers sorts flourishing and green all the Year." [20] Its people lack energy, perhaps because they have no roads; it may be equally true that they lack roads because they have no energy. However this may be, the province can and some day will grow coffee, tobacco, rice, and cocoa to perfection; its savannahs will furnish pasturage for thousands of cattle, where now some one solitary *carabao* serves only to mark the solitude in which he stands.

We crossed the stream about seven in the morning, May 1, and opened out on an immense field, which we estimated at about thirty-five hundred acres, a whole plantation in a ring fence, and offering not the slightest suggestion of the tropics in its aspect. The ground now broke and we went on down to a bold stream so deep that those of us riding ponies got wet above the knees and were almost swept down by the current. The *cogon* grass in this river bottom was the tallest I ever saw, some clumps being well over twenty feet high. Then we began to climb till we reached another divide, across the stream at the foot of which was Payawan, our immediate objective. Payawan consists of two shacks and a name. Here we were to have had our first meeting with the clans of the Ifugao, but through some misunderstanding they took the place of meeting to be at Kiangan, some, miles further on; so we all rested a while, and some of us took a swim in the little river we had just crossed, finding the water on first shock almost cold, but delightful beyond belief. Cootes and I were quite satisfied with the pool we found near the shack, but Strong and the rest thought they saw a better one downstream, so they crawled in the water around a small cliff, reached their pool, and then had to walk a mile and a half through the *cogon* and in the sun to return, there being no getting back upstream. Now, if there is anything else hotter on the face of the earth than a walk through the *cogon* in the dry season with the sun shining vertically down, it has yet to be discovered.

At Payawan we were met by Captain Jeff D. Gallman, P. C, Lieutenant-Governor of the Sub-province of Ifugao, accompanied by one of his chieftains, who made a splendid picture in his barbaric finery. Erect, thin of flank and well-muscled, he had a bold, clear eye and a fearless look; around his neck he wore a complicated necklace of gold and other beads; each upper arm was clasped by a boar's tusk, from which stood out a plume of red horse-hair. His gee-string was decorated with a belt of white shells, the long free end hanging down in front, and he had his bolo, like the rest of his people, in a half-scabbard - that is, kept by two straps on a strip of wood, shaped like a scabbard. But all these were mere accessories; what distinguished him was his free graceful carriage, the lightness and ease of his motions, the frankness and openness of his countenance.

Our rest over, we pushed on through a beautiful forest, unlike any other seen so far in that it was open. The trail was excellent, and rose steadily, for we had to cross a sharp range before making Kiangan. I shall make no attempt to describe this exquisite afternoon: but there was a breeze, the forest tempered the sun's rays a good part of the time; and, as we rose, range after range, peak on peak opened on our view, valley after valley spread out under our feet until I wearied of admiring. The others had gone over the trail before, and looked on nature with a more matter-of-fact eye. At the top of the range I noticed an outcrop of fossil coral. Bubud distinguished himself to-day. Gallman, who was trotting immediately in front (and who ought to know his own trails!), called "Ware hole!" just as Bubud put one of his forefeet in it, pitched forward, and threw me over his head, thus establishing a complete breach of continuity between us. However, as long as the thing had to happen, it was a good place to select, for the trail was four feet wide here, and, in case of going over the side, the drop was only eighty or ninety feet, with bushes conveniently arranged to catch hold of on the way down. This was Bubud's solitary mishap, and it was not his fault.

Past the divide, the trail became a road over which one

might have marched a field battery, so broad and firm and good was it: we were nearing Kiangan. Presently we turned a low spur to the left, and the Ifugao town burst upon our view. It was the headquarters of a Spanish *Comandancia* in the old days, and here Padre Juan Villaverde lived and worked, seeking to convert the people, and to teach them to grow coffee and to plant European vegetables. The mission, however came to naught, leaving behind no trace visible to the casual traveller, save a few lone cabbages: the garrison maintained here was massacred to a man, the native who surprised and cut down the sentry being pointed out to us the next day. Kiangan was celebrated in Spanish times, and even more recently, as the home of some of the most desperate head-hunters of the Archipelago. But, thanks to Gallman, head-hunting in the Ifugao country is now a thing of the past.

The town stands on the top of a bastion-like terrace, thrust avalanche-wise and immense between its pinnacled mountain walls; the site is not only of great beauty, but of great natural strength, like nearly all the other considerable settlements we saw on this journey. The two mountain walls approach somewhat like the branches of the letter V, having between them, near their intersection, as it were, the natural bastion mentioned rising from the bed of the Ibilao River, hundreds of feet below, and some thousands of yards distant. The whole position is on a large generous scale; it would have appealed to the ancient Greeks. And so, of course, we yet had some distance to go, and now made our way through rice-paddies, echeloned on the flanks of the spurs that came down to meet us. These rice-terraces (*sementeras*), the first I had seen, at once excited my interest, to the scorn of Pack, who bade me wait until we had come upon the real thing:

these were nothing. It turned out he was entirely right; but I thought them remarkable, and anyway they were most refreshing and cooling to look at, after our long hot ride. The sound of running waters, the sight of the little runlets bubbling away for dear life, of the tall rice swaying to the breeze, the acropolis before us with its clumps of waving bamboos, of nodding bananas, and the soft afternoon light over all, the combination made a picture that, will live in my recollection. The impression immediately formed was that of a scene of quiet peace and beauty, more or less rudely shocked the following day. As we drew nearer and nearer we were welcomed by arches of bamboo decorated with native flowers and plants, and guarded by life-size *anitos* [21] of both sexes *in puris naturalibus*, cut out of the tree fern, but with no connotation whatever of indecency. For these statues are either an innocent expression of nature, or, what seems more likely, an expression of Nature or phallic worship.

We had now got up to the parade of the *cuartel* (quarters or barracks) and were greeted by shouts from the people gathered to welcome us. The chief who had met us at Payawan, and who, on foot, had beaten us into Kiangan, appeared in all his bravery and with a prolonged "Who-o-o-o-e-e!" commanded silence. He then mounted a bamboo stand some twenty feet high, with a platform on top, and made us a speech! Yes, a regular speech, with gestures, intonations, and all the rest of it. For these Ifugaos are born orators, and love to show their skill. Accordingly, thanks to Mr. Worcester's appreciation, orators' tribunes have been put up at points like Kiangan; it is strange that the Ifugaos had never thought of it themselves. This tribune, by the way, was ornamented with tufts of leaves and grasses at the corners. When the speaker had done, he clapped his hands over his head, and all the people followed suit.

Later on Gallman, who speaks Ifugao like a native, interpreted for us. The speaker told his people that a great honor had been done them by this visit of the "Commission," and that, besides, the great *apo* [22] of all had come, too. His arrival could not fail to be of good luck for them, as it meant more rice, more chickens, more pigs, more babies, more good in all ways than they ever had had before. As other speeches began to threaten, on a hasty intimation from Mr. Forbes we moved on to our quarters, preceded by the escort of Constabulary.

This detachment, composed entirely of Ifugaos, would have delighted any soldier. They certainly excited my admiration by the precision of their movements, their set-up, and their general appearance. A Prussian Guardsman could not have been more erect. There are five companies of Constabulary in the Mountain Province, each serving in the part of the country from which recruited, and each retaining in its uniform the colors and such other native features as could be turned to account. Thus the only "civilized," so to say, elements are the forage cap and khaki jacket worn directly over the skin; otherwise the legs, feet, and body are bare; the local gee-string is worn, with the free end hanging down in front. Here at Kiangan each man has below the knee the native brass leglet, and on the left hip the *bultong*, or native bag, a sporran, indeed, showing the local influence in its blue and white stripes. Thus accoutered, the first impression formed was that these troops were actually highlanders; on reflection, this impression is correct, for they are highlanders in every sense of the word. I

Cornelis De Witt Willcox

obtained permission to inspect the detachment after the honors were over, and found their equipment and uniforms in admirable condition. Of their discipline, everyone spoke in the highest terms; indeed, we had next day, as will soon appear, an example of this quality. Their loyalty to the Government is unquestioned. These mountaineers are all, as might be expected, hardy, strong, able-bodied, and active; in fact, the physical qualities of these mountain people are remarkable. But at Kiangan, as elsewhere, it was noticeable that discipline, regular habits, regular food, had improved the naturally good physical qualities of the people. The Constabulary appeared to me to be physically better than the tribe from which they were drawn. I noticed, too, that after protracted wearing of the khaki the skin of the body was several shades lighter than that of the legs.

We now entered our quarters, being those of Lieutenant Meimban, the native officer in command. Here, too, we met Mr. Barton, the local school superintendent. His predecessor had had to be relieved, because one day, as he was going up the trail, an Ifugao threw a spear "into" him, as they say in the mountains, and he consequently got a sort of distaste for the place, although it was clearly established in the investigation that followed, and carefully explained to him, that it was all a mistake, and that the spear had been intended for somebody else. Mr. Barton is doing a useful work here in devoting his spare time and energy to a study of the Ifugao religion with its myths and mythology. He told me that he had so far defined seven hundred different spirits and was not sure that he had got to the end of them. The publication of Mr. Barton's research is awaited with some avidity by the Americans living in the Province , as enabling them to have a better control of the people through their religious beliefs.

We had not long been seated in our quarters before a deputation of chiefs with their *gansas* and a large number of *bubud* [23] jars entered, and offered us *bubud* to drink. Very soon our visitors began to dance for us to the sound of the *gansa*, their dance being different from that we had seen a few days before at Campote. As, however, the next day was one dance from morning to night, I shall not spend any more time upon this affair, except to say that, turn about being fair play, Cootes got up and gave such a representation as he was able of a *pas seul*. When he had done, our visitors started anew, and the *gansas* proving irresistible, Cootes and I joined in. The steps, poise of body, motion of the arms and hands are so marked and peculiar that a little observation and practice enabled us in a short time to produce at least a fair imitation; indeed, so successful were our efforts that we were informed we should be invited to dance on the morrow before the multitudes! This brought us up standing, and it was time anyway. So our chieftains took their leave, their *bubud* jars remaining in our charge. These jars are worth more than a passing mention: the oldest ones come from China, and are held in such high esteem by the Ifugaos that they will part with them for neither love nor money. According to the experts, some of them are examples of the earliest known forms of Chinese porcelain, and are most highly prized by collectors and museums. [24]

We put up our mosquito-bars this night, the only time on the trip, but I think without any necessity. So far we had not seen, heard or felt a single fly or mosquito, and were to see none until we struck civilization once more in the Cagayan Valley.

Cornelis De Witt Willcox

CHAPTER XII

Day opens badly. - Ifugao houses. - The people,
assemble. - Dancing. - Speeches. - White paper
streamers. - Head hunter dance. - Canao.

Needless to say we were up betimes the next morning,
May 2d, for the clans were to gather, and the day
would hardly be long enough for all it was to hold. The
day began ominously. As Kiangan is a sort of
headquarters, it has a guard-house for the service of
short imprisonments, a post-and-rail affair made of
bamboo under the *cuartel*. For while our administration is kindly, these mountaineers from the first have
had to learn, if not to feel as yet, that they must be
punished if guilty of infringing such laws and
discipline as have so far been found applicable.
Accordingly, our guard-house held two men, sentenced
for twenty days, for having threatened the life of one of
their head men. Short as was the sentence, these two
men had nevertheless dug a passage in the earthen
floor of their quarters, and had just the night before
opened the outer end of it, but not enough to admit the
passage of a human body. A private of Constabulary,
passing by this morning, stooped to examine this hole
new to him, when one of the prisoners threw a spear at
him, made of a stalk of *runo* [25] the head being a
small strip of iron which he had kept concealed in his
gee-string. So true was his aim that, although he had to
throw his improvised spear between the rails, he

nevertheless struck the private in the neck, cutting his jugular vein, so that in five minutes he was dead. The pen was now entered for the purpose of shackling the criminal, when he announced that he would kill any white man that laid hands on him. Upon Lieutenant Meimban of the Constabulary advancing, both of the prisoners rushed him. In the mellay that followed the murderer was shot and killed and his companion badly beaten up; Strong later had to put seventeen stitches in one scalp wound alone. Although the *rancheria* from which the murdered private came was two hours off, so that it usually took four hours to send a message and get an answer, yet an hour and a half after the man died a runner came in to ask for his body so it could be suitably buried. Altogether, this double killing damped our spirits considerably; for one thing, there was no telling how it would be received, particularly if there should be any excessive drinking of *buhud*; there were very few of us, mostly unarmed, and the Ifugaos were coming in hundreds at a time, so that long before the forenoon was well under way several thousands had collected. However, on moving out, we could not find that the cheerfulness of the people had been in the least disturbed.

Before beginning the business of the day we walked about the village and examined one or two houses. These are all of one room, entered by a ladder drawn up at night, and set up on stout posts seven or eight feet high; the roof is thatched, and the walls, made of wattle *(suali)*, flare out from the base determined by the tops of the posts. In cutting the posts down to suitable size (say 10 inches in diameter), a flange, or collar, is left near the top to keep rats out; chicken-coops hang around, and formerly human skulls, too, were set about. But the Ifugaos, thanks to Gallman, as already said, have abandoned head-hunting, and the skulls in hand, if kept at all, are now hidden inside their owner's houses, their places being taken by carabao heads and horns. One house had a *tahibi*, or rest-couch; only rich people can own these, cut out as they are of a single log, in longitudinal cross-section like an inverted and very flat V with suitable head- and foot-supports. The notable who wishes to own one of these luxurious couches gets his friends to cut down the tree (which is necessarily of very large size), to haul the log, and to carve out the couch, feeding them the while. Considering the lack of tools, trails, and animals, the labor must be incredible and the cost enormous. However, wealth will have its way in Kiangan as well as in Paris.

By the time we had done the village, the hour of business had come, and we moved up to the little parade in front of the *cuartel*, where an enormous crowd had already assembled. As at Campote, so here, and for the same reasons, very few old women were present, but about as many young ones and children as there were men. Our approach was the signal for the dancing to begin, and once begun, it lasted all day, the *gansas* never ceasing their invitation. Apparently anybody could join in, and many did, informal circles being formed here and there, for the Ifugaos, like all the other highlanders, dance around in a circle. Both men and women took part, eyes on a point of the ground a yard or so ahead, the knees a little bent, left foot in front, body slightly forward on the hips, left arm out in front, hand upstretched with fingers joined, right arm akimbo, with hand behind right hip. The musicians kneel, stick the forked-stick handle of the *gansa* in their gee-strings, with the *gansa* convex side up on their thighs, and use both hands, the right sounding the note with a downward stroke, the left serving to damp the sound. The step is a very dignified, slow shuffle, accompanied by slow turns and twists of the left hand, and a peculiar and rapid up-and-down motion of the right.

True to what had been said the day before, a particularly large circle was formed, and Cootes and I were invited to join, which we did; if any conclusion may be drawn from the applause we got (for the Ifugaos clap hands), why, modesty apart, we upheld the honor of the Service.

Every now and then the orators had their turn, for a resounding "Whoo-o-ee!" would silence the multitudes, and some speaker would mount the tribune and give vent to an impassioned discourse. One of these bore on the killing of the prisoner that morning: the orator declared that he was a bad man, and that he had met with a just end, that the people must understand that they must behave themselves properly, and so on. I forget how many speeches were made; but the tribune was never long unoccupied. Another performance of the day was the distribution of strips of white onion-skin paper. On one of his previous trips Mr. Worcester had noticed that the people had taken an old newspaper he had brought with him, cut it up into strips, and tied them to the hair by way of ornament. Acting on this hint, it is his habit to take with him on his trips to this country thousands of strips, and everybody gets a share according to rank, a chief five, his wife four, an ordinary person three, and little children two. Accordingly, he spent hours this day handing out these strips, for this was a duty that could not be delegated: the strips must come from the hands of the "Commission" himself. By afternoon, every man, woman, and child - and there were thousands of them all told - was flying these white streamers from the head, the combined resulting effect being pleasing and graceful. Meanwhile the people kept on coming from their *rancherias*, one arrival creating something of a stir, being that of the *Princesa*, wife of the orator who had welcomed us the day before. She came in state, reclining in a sort of bag hanging from a bamboo borne on the shoulders of some of her followers. She had an umbrella, and, if I recollect aright, was smoking a cigar. On emerging from her bag, a circle formed about her, and she was graciously pleased to dance for us, no one venturing to join her. As she was fat and scant o' breath, [26] her performance, was characterized by portentous deliberation, precision, and dignity, and was as palpably agreeable to her as it was curious to us.

The great performance of the morning, however, was a head-hunter dance, arranged by Barton; that is, he had gone out a day or two before and told a neighboring *rancheria*, that they must furnish a show of the sort for the *apos* whose visit was imminent. But, according to the old women of the village, he had made a great mistake in that he said it was not necessary to hold a *canao* in advance. A *canao* (*buni* in Ifugao), as already explained, is a ceremonious occasion, celebrated by dancing, much drinking of *bubud*, the killing of a pig, speeches. Whenever an affair of moment is in hand, such as a funeral or a head-hunting expedition, a *canao* is held. Our entire stay at Kiangan might be called a *canao*, or, rather, it was made up of *canaos*. Now when Barton, two or three days before, refused to *canao*, the old women shook their heads, declaring that something would happen, and the killings of the morning were at once summoned as proof that they were right and he was wrong. However this may be, not long after the

Princesa's dance we heard below us a cadenced sound and saw a long column in file slowly approaching. Its head was formed of warriors armed with spears and shields stained black with white zig-zags across; the leading warrior walked backward, continually making thrusts at the next man with his spear. A pig had immediately preceded, trussed by his feet to a bamboo, and interfering mightily with the music that followed. This was percussive in character, and was produced by twenty-five or thirty men beating curved instruments, made of very hard, resonant wood, with sticks. These musicians marched along almost doubled over, and would lean in unison first to the right and then to the left, striking first one end, then the other of their instruments, which they held in the middle by a *bejuco* string from a hole made for the purpose. The note was not unmusical. Many of the men had their head-baskets on their backs, and one or two of them the palm-leaf rain-coat. I had never imagined that it was possible for human beings to advance as slowly as did these warriors; in respect of speed, our most dignified funerals would suffer by comparison. The truth is, they were dancing. They got up the hill at last, however; laid the pig down in the middle of the vast circle that had instantly formed, and then began the ceremonious head-dance. Two or three men, after various words had been said, would march around in stately fashion, winding up at the pig, across whose body they would lay their spears. On this an old man would run out, and remove the spears, when the thing would be repeated. At last, a tall, handsome young man, splendidly turned out in all his native embellishments, on reaching the pig, allowed his companions to retire while he himself stood, and, facing his party with a smile, said a few words. Then, without looking at his victim, and without ceasing to speak, he suddenly thrust his spear into the pig's heart, withdrawing it so quickly that the blade remained unstained with blood; as quick and accurate a thing as ever seen! Of course, this entire *canao* was full of meaning to the initiated. Barton said it was a failure, and he ought to know; but it was very interesting to us. I was particularly struck by the bearing of these men, their bold, free carriage and fearless expression of countenance.

CHAPTER XIII

Dress of the people. - Butchery of carabao. - Prisoner
runs *amok* and is killed.

It was now drawing near midday, and as though by
common understanding we all separated to get
something to eat. Our head-dancers formed up and
resumed their slow march back down the hill; only this
time, Cootes and I borrowed instruments and joined
the band, partly to see how it felt to walk in so
incredibly slow a procession, and partly for me, at
least, to try the music. A little of it went a long way.

The afternoon was, with two exceptions, much like the
forenoon. Tiffin over, Mr. Worcester and Gallman held
councils with the head men of the various *rancherias*
present; Pack inspected; and the rest of us moved
about, looking on at whatever interested us.

As elsewhere, but few clothes are seen: the women
wear a short striped skirt sarong-wise, but bare the
bosom. However, they are beginning to cover it, just as
a few of them had regular umbrellas. They leave the
navel uncovered; to conceal it would be immodest. The
men are naked save the gee-string, unless a leglet of
brass wire under the knee be regarded as a garment;
the bodies of many of them are tattooed in a leaf-like
pattern. A few men had the native blanket hanging
from their shoulders, but leaving the body bare in

front. The prevailing color is blue; at Campote it is red. The hair looked as though a bowl had been clapped on the head at an angle of forty-five degrees, and all projecting locks cut off. If the hair is long, it means that the wearer has made a vow to let it grow until he has killed someone or burnt an enemy's house. We saw such a long-haired man this day. Some of the men wore over their gee-strings belts made of shell (mother-of-pearl), with a long free end hanging down in front. These belts are very costly and highly thought of. Earrings are common, but apparently the lobe of the ear is not unduly distended. Here at Kiangan, the earring consists of a spiral of very fine brass wire.

It is pertinent to remark that the Ifugaos treat their women well; for example, the men do the heavy work, and there are no women *cargadores*. In fact, the sexes seemed to me to be on terms of perfect equality. The people in general appeared to be cheerful, good-humored, and hospitable. Mr. Worcester pointed out that whereas most of the men present were unarmed (at any rate, they had neither spears nor shields), in his early trips through this country, as elsewhere, every man came on fully armed, and the ground was stuck full of spears, each with its shield leaning on it, the owner near by with the rest of his *rancheria*, and all ready at a moment's notice to kill and take heads. For although these people are all of the same blood and speak nearly the same language, still there is no tribal government; the people live in independent settlements (*rancherias*), all as recently as five or six years ago hostile to one another, and taking heads at every opportunity. This state of affairs was undoubtedly partly due to the almost complete lack of communication then prevailing, thus limiting the activities of each *rancheria* to the growing of food, varied by an effort to take as many heads as possible from the *rancheria* across the valley, without undue loss of its own. And what is said here of the Ifugao is true also of the Ilongot, the Igorot, the Kalinga, the Apayao, and of all the rest of the head-hunting highlanders of Northern Luzon. The results accomplished by Mr. Worcester with all these people simply exceed belief. But this subject, being worthy of more than passing mention, will be considered later. The afternoon is wearing on, and we must get at the two exceptions mentioned some little time ago.

Since these highlanders have but little meat to eat, it is the policy of the Government, on the occasion of these annual progresses, to furnish a few carabaos, so that some of the people, at least, while they are the guests of the Government, may have what they are fondest of and most infrequently get. And they have been until recently allowed to slaughter the carabao, according to their own custom, in competition, catch-as-catch-can, so to say. For the poor beast, tethered and eating grass all unconscious of its fate, or else directly led out, is surrounded by a mob of men and boys, each with his bolo. At a signal given, the crowd rushes on the animal, and each man hacks and cuts at the part nearest to him, the rule of the game being that any part cut off must be carried out of the rush and deposited on the ground before it can become the bearer's property. Accordingly, no sooner is a piece separated and brought out than it is pounced on by others who try to take it away; usually a division takes place, subject to further sub-division, however, if other claimants are at hand. The competition is not only tremendous, but dangerous, for in their excitement the contestants frequently wound one another. The Government (*i.e.*, Mr. Worcester), while at first necessarily allowing this sort of butchering, has steadily discouraged and gradually reduced it, so that at Kiangan, for example, the people were told that this was the last time they would ever be allowed to kill beef in this fashion. It was pointed out to them that the purpose being to furnish meat, their method of killing was so uneconomical that the beef was really ruined, and nobody got what he was really entitled to.

On this occasion, the carabao was tied to a stake in a small swale and I nerved myself to look on. I saw the first cuts, the poor beast look up from his grass in astonishment, totter, reel, and fall as blows rained on him from all sides. The crowd, closing in, mercifully hid the rest from view; the victim dying game without a sound. In this respect, as well as in many others, the carabao is a very different animal from the pig. But, while looking on at the mound of cutting, hacking, sweating, and struggling butchers, the smell of fresh blood over all, something occurred that completely shifted the center of interest. A boy came up to us in great excitement to say that the prisoner had got hold of a bayonet and was running *amok*. This was the prisoner of the morning who had been so badly beaten; to make him more comfortable, he had been laid on the veranda of the *cuartel* (just behind us), hobbled, but otherwise free. The boy spoke the truth; the prisoner had snatched his bayonet from a passing Constabulary private, and, turning into the *cuartel*, made for the provincial treasurer, who was busy inside. Him he chased out, getting over the ground with extraordinary rapidity, considering his wounds and hobbles; when we turned to look, the prisoner had come out and was running for just anybody. There was now but one thing to do, and done it was. Some one in authority called out to the sentry on duty before the *cuartel*. "Kill him!"

The sentry, who up to this time had been walking up and down as a sentry should, brought down his carbine, aimed at the running man, and dropped him in his tracks by a bullet through the heart. He then ejected his empty cartridge-case, shouldered his piece, and continued to walk his post as unconcernedly as though he had shot a mad dog; as striking an example of discipline as any soldier could wish to see. So far as I could mark, this occurrence made no impression on the people gathered together. The day went on as before. We should recollect, however, that these highlanders have no nerves, have, in the the past held human life cheap, and must have realized in this case that the poor fellow who had been shot was himself trying to take human life; according to mountain law, he had got his deserts. Hence no astonishment should be felt that, while this human tragedy was being played to a finish, the carabao-butchers had not turned a hair's breadth from their business. For when I turned again to see how they were getting on, I found that they had disappeared, and, walking to the place, saw not a trace of the butchery save the trampled ground and a small heap of undigested grass. Mr. Worcester had told me before that I should find this to be the case; not a shred of hoof, hide , or bone had been left behind.

The multitude had now begun to disperse, for the sun's rays were growing level, and the day was over. We were glad ourselves to find our quarters, for we had had some ten hours of *gansa*-beating, dancing, and all the rest of it: the *canao* had been a great success, and, although *bubud* had passed vigorously, the people had made no trouble. We wound up with a little bridge, and there was, as there always is, some business to be dispatched before turning in. But we were all soon sound asleep, for next morning we had to be up at four. [27]

CHAPTER XIV

Barton's account of a native funeral.

Mr. Barton, already mentioned as in residence at Kiangan as local Superintendent of Schools, went out to see the funeral of the Constabulary private killed on the morning of the 2d. He was strongly advised not to go, because these highlanders resent more or less the presence of strangers at their funeral ceremonies. But this made him only the more eager, as very few Americans, or any others for that matter, have ever been present on these occasions.

Passing through Manila a month or two later, he very kindly dictated for me an account of what he saw, and I give it here, with his permission, in his own words:

The Funeral of Aliguyen.

"On the third day after the soldier was killed, the principal funeral ceremonies took place. To these ceremonies came a great number of people from their various *rancherias*, the party from each *rancheria* being led by the relatives of the soldier, some of them very distant relatives.

"Aliguyen, the dead soldier, lived in the *rancheria* of Nagukaran, a *rancheria* until quite recently very unfriendly to Kiangan, where I live. Aliguyen, however, had some kin in Kiangan, and this kin, together with their friends, went to the funeral. Their shields, as well as the shields of all who attended, were painted with white markings, taking some the form of men, some of lizards, some were zig-zags. All men who attended had a head-dress made of the leaf petiole of the betel tree and the red leaves of the dongola plant. To these leaves were attached pendant white feathers. Everybody was dressed in his best clout, and the women in their best loin-cloths and in all their finery of gold beads and agate necklaces.

"Nagukaran is one *rancheria* of several in a very large valley. When I reached a point in the trail commanding this valley, there could be seen from various *rancherias* in the valley a procession from each of them wending their way slowly toward Aliguyen's home. From the time that they came within sight of the house, which was sometimes when they were a mile and a half or two miles from it, each procession danced its way, beating on the striped shields with their drum-sticks and on their *bangibang*. This last is a kind of wooden stick, made of resonant hard wood, coated over with chicken blood. It is extremely old. It is curved slightly and is about two feet long, and is held in one hand suspended by a *bejuco* string so that the vibrations are not interfered with. It is beaten with a drum-stick, as is also the shield. The *gansa*, or brass gong, the usual musical instrument of the Ifugaos, is never used in the funeral of a beheaded man. The two men who headed each procession carried two spears each. Behind came a man carrying a spear and shield. The two in front faced the on-coming procession, stepping most of the time backward, making thrusts toward the two who bore the spears and shields. The bearers of spear and shield made thrusts at them, the whole being a dance which in some respects resembles one of the head-dances of the Bontoc Igorots. From the high place on the trail where I was, they looked, in the distance, like nothing so much as columns of centipedes or files of ants all creeping slowly along the dikes of the rice-paddies toward the central place. It usually takes an hour for such a procession to cover one mile. The beating of shield and stick could easily be heard across the wide valley on that still morning.

"Arriving at Aliguyen's house, we found him sitting on a block facing the sun, lying against his shield, which was supported by the side of the house. The body was in a terrible state of decomposition. It was swollen to three times its living girth. Great blisters had collected under the epidermis, which broke from time to time, a brownish red fluid escaping. The spear wound in his neck was plugged by a wooden spear-head. In each hand Aliguyen held a wooden spear. No attempt whatever had been made to prevent decomposition of the body or the entrance to it of flies. From the mouth gas bubbled out continually. Two old women on each side with penholder-shaped loom-sticks about two feet long continually poked at Aliguyen's face and the wound to wake him up. From time to time they caught the grewsome head by the hair and shook it violently, shouting, Who-oo-oo! Aliguyen, wake up! Open your eyes! Look down on Kurug. [Kurug being the *rancheria* from which came Aliguyen's murderer.] Take his father and his mother, his wife and his children, and his first cousins and his second cousins, and his relatives by marriage. They wanted him to kill you. All your kin are women. [They say this in order to deceive Aliguyen into avenging himself.] They can't avenge you. You will have to avenge yourself! There

Cornelis De Witt Willcox

is *orden* [law]; no one can kill them but you! Take them all!

"This calling on Aliguyen's soul never ceased. When an old woman got hoarse, another took her place. As the procession came to the house it filed past Aliguyen and its leaders stopped and shouted words to the same effect. The key-note of the whole ceremony was vengeance. It is true that both persons who were involved in killing Aliguyen were themselves killed, but the people of a *rancheria* regard themselves as being about the only real people in the world and hold that three, four, or five men of another *rancheria* are not equal to one of theirs.

"Nagukaran being the *rancheria* that speared and nearly killed my predecessor, Mr. - , I explained my presence to the people there by saying that the soldier, being an agent of our Government, was in a way a relative of mine. The explanation was a perfectly natural one to the people, and they treated me with the greatest courtesy and helped me to see whatever was to be seen.

"Toward noon they told me that they were going to perform the feast which looked towards securing vengeance for Aliguyen's death. They went to where the people had built a shed to protect them from the sun's fierce rays on a little hillock some distance from any house. Two pigs were provided there, one being very small. Only the old men were permitted to gather around the pigs and the rice-wine and the other appurtenances of the feast. The feast began by a prayer to the ancestors, followed by an invocation to the various deities. The most interesting and the principal part of the feast was the invocation to the celestial bodies, who are believed to be the deities of War and Justice, Manahaut (The Deceiver), a companion of the Sun God, was first invoked. The people cried: Whoo-oo-oo! Manahaut, look down! Come down and drink the rice-wine and take the pig! Don't deceive us! Deceive our enemies! Take them into the remotest quarters of the sky-world; lock them up there forever so that they may not return! Vengeance for him who has gone before!' Then an old man put his hands over his forehead and called: 'Come down, Manahaut.' Manahaut came and possessed him, causing him to call out: 'Sa-ay! sa-ay! I come down Manahaut; I drink the rice-wine; I will deceive your enemies, but I will not deceive you,' The old man, possessed, jumps up and, with characteristic Ifugao dance step, dances about the rice-wine jar and about the pig. Quickly follows him a feaster who has called Umalgo, the Spirit of the Sun, and was possessed by him. Manahaut dances ahead of Umalgo to show him the pig. Umalgo seizes a spear, dances about the pig two or three times, when he steps over to it and with a thrust, seemingly without effort, pierces its heart. The blood spurts out of the pig's side and there quickly follows a feaster who has been possessed by Umbulan, who throws himself on the pig and drinks its blood. He would remain there forever, say the people, drinking the pig's blood, were it not that one of the Stars, his son, possesses a feaster, causing him to dance over to Umbulan, catch him by the hair and lead him from the pig. Following these ceremonies, there came feasters of various spirits of the Stars to cut the pig's feet and his head off. Then comes the cutting up of the pig to cook in the pots. The blood that has settled in its chest is carefully caught; it is used to smear the *bangibang* and the *jipag*. The *jipag* are interesting. They are little images of two or three of the deities that help men to take heads. The

Cornelis De Witt Willcox

images are of wood about six or eight inches high. Sometimes there are images of dogs also. When an Ifugao goes on a head-hunting expedition, he takes the images in his head-basket, together with a stone to make the enemy's feet heavy so that he cannot run away, and a little wooden stick in representation of a spear, to the end of which is attached a stone - this to make the enemy's spear strike the earth so that it might not strike him. [28]

"As the pig was being put in the pot to be cooked for the old men who had performed the feast, some unmannerly young fellow started to make away with one piece of the flesh. Immediately there was a scramble which was joined by some three or four hundred Ifugaos of all the different *rancherias*. Then the feasters (I think there were about one thousand who attended the feast) leaped for their spears and shields. The people who had come from Kiangan rushed to where I was and took their stand in front of and around me, and told me to stay there and that they would protect me from any harm; all of which, as may well be supposed, produced no trifling amount of warmth in my feelings toward them. Fortunately nothing came of the scramble.

"I have no hesitancy in saying that two or three years ago, before Governor Gallman had performed his excellent and truly wonderful work among the Ifugaos, this scramble would have become a fight in which somebody would have lost his life. That such a thing could take place without danger was incomprehensible to the old women of Kiangan, who doubtless remembered sons or husbands, brothers or cousins, who had lost their lives in such an affair. With the memory of these old times in their minds they caught me by the arms and by the waist and said, 'Barton, come home; we don't know the mind of the people; they are likely to kill you.' When I refused to miss seeing the rest of the feast, they told me to keep my revolver ready.

"Looking back on this incident, I am sure that I was in little, I believe *no* danger, but must give credit to my Ifugao boy who attended me in having the wisest head in the party. This boy immediately thought of my horse, which was picketed near, and ran to it, taking with him one or two responsible Kiangan men to help him watch and defend it. Had he not done so, some meat-hungry, hot-headed Ifugao might easily have stuck a bolo in his side during the scramble and its confusion; and immediately some five hundred or more Ifugaos would have been right on top of the carcase, hand-hacking at it with their long war-knives, and it would probably have been impossible ever to find out who gave the first thrust.

"The old men who had performed the feast, after things had quieted down somewhat, began scolding and cursing those who had run away with the meat. Finally they managed to prevail upon the meat-snatchers to bring back three small pieces, about the size of their hands, from which I concluded that Ifugao is a language which is admirably adapted to making people ashamed of themselves. For I knew how hungry for meat these Ifugao become.

"Three old men stuck their spears in a piece of meat and began a long story whose text was the confusion of enemies in some past time. At the conclusion of each story, they said: 'Not there, but here; not then, but now.' By a sort of simple witchcraft, the mere telling of these stories is believed to secure a like confusion and

Cornelis De Witt Willcox

destruction of the enemies of the present. When this ceremony had been completed, each old man raised his spear quickly and so was enabled to secure for himself the meat impaled. In one case, one of the old men just missed ripping open the abdomen of the man who stood in front.

"The feast being finished, the people made an attempt to assemble by *rancherias*. Then they filed along the trail to bury Aliguyen. Nagukaran *rancheria* took the lead. As the procession came near the grave the men took off their head-dresses and strung them on a long pole, which was laid across the trail. A Nagukaran *ranchero* went to where Aliguyen was sitting and picked him up, carried him to the grave, and placed him in a sitting posture facing Kurug, the *rancheria* that killed him, Aliguyen was not wrapped in a death-blanket, as corpses usually are. His body was neglected in order to make him angry, so to incite him to vengeance.

"The grave was a kind of sepulchre dug out of a bank. It was walled up with stones after Aliguyen was placed in it, and an egg thrown against the tomb, whereupon the people yelled: '*Batna kana okukulan di bujolmi ud Kurug!* ('So may it happen to our enemies at Kurug!') The poles on which were strung the head-dresses were taken and hung over the door of Aliguyen's house. After this the people dispersed to their homes. On the way home they stopped at a stream and washed themselves, praying somewhat as follows: 'Wash, Water, but do not wash away our lives, our pigs, our chickens, our rice, our children. Wash away death by violence, death by the spear, death by sickness. Wash away pests, hunger, and crop-failure, and our enemies. Wash away the visits of the Spear-bearing Nightcomer, the Mountain Haunters, the Ghosts, the Westcomers. Wash away our enemies. Wash as vengeance for him who has gone before.'"

Cornelis De Witt Willcox

CHAPTER XV

Visit to the Silipan Ifugaos at Andangle. - The Ibilao River. - Athletic feat. - Rest-house and stable at Sabig.

We set out the next day, May 3d, at dawn, our destination being Andangle, selected as a rendezvous of the Silipan Ifugaos, another branch of the great tribe under Gallman's domination. And, to my great regret, we here parted from Connor, who had accompanied us thus far, but now had to return to his post in Nueva Vizcaya. I have the greatest pleasure in acknowledging here his many courtesies, the good humor and patience with which he answered my many questions, and I hated to see him turn back.

The trail we were to take to-day was most of it new, the Silipan Ifugaos having finished it but a short time before our arrival. We rode through the reddening dawn, down the great bastion of Kiangan, with the Ibilao River, far below us, showing now and then on the turn of a spur, till at last it uncovered so much of its length as lay in the valley, and disappearing to the southeast through its tremendous gates of rock. For the everlasting mountains, narrowing down on each side, as though to halt the impetuous stream, nevertheless yield it passage through smooth, vertical walls of solid rock, a gate never closed, nor yet ever open. It would have been most interesting to work our way down to this example of Nature's engineering, but we had to content ourselves with a look from afar, and soon the trail turned sharply to the left and shut out the view. The whole valley was keen that morning with its fresh, cool air and sound of rushing waters. It was a happiness to be alive, up, and riding.

In about half an hour we reached the right bank of the river, where we off-saddled, crossing by a trolley platform; the horses were swum over, and the kit carried by the *cargadores* on their heads. My *cargador* must have gone down, for when I got my gear later it was soaking wet. On the other side we began to climb, and sharply; we now could look back on Kiangan. Rounding the nose of a gigantic, buttress-like spur, covered with *camote* patches, we descended to a small affluent of the Ibilao, where we halted and rested, and, crossing it, again began to climb, the trail being cut out of the side of another gigantic spur. At last we reached the top, to find a new deep, steep valley below us, and just across, only a few parasangs away, Andangle. But it was far more than a few parasangs by the trail, for we had to go completely around the head of the valley, mostly on the same contour. Andangle itself is barely more than a name, but we found here a house of bamboo and palm fresh built for us, tastefully adorned with greens and plants, and protected by *anitos*, resembling those of Kiangan. Like nearly all the other places visited by us, it was finely situated, the mountains we had just ridden through forming a great amphitheater to the north.

Our stay here was uneventful. There is really little to record or report. This branch of the Ifugaos impressed me as being a quieter [29] lot than the people we had just left and apparently fonder, if possible, of speech-making. For speeches went on almost without intermission, all breathing good-will and declaring the intention of the people to behave in a lawful manner and promising to have done with killing and stealing.

There were many women and children, the children very shy. Of weapons there were none. Dancing went on uninterruptedly the whole day and night of our stay, and Cootes and I had to dance again. Only we had now arranged to simulate a boxing-match, which we presented to the beat of the *gansa*, and to the applause of our gallery. A runner came in while we were here, carrying a note in a cleft stick, the native substitute for a pocket. In dress and appearance, the Andangle people differed in no wise from those of Kiangan. Many of them, however, have a silver jewel, of curious and original design, worn chiefly as earring, but also on a string around the neck. Our splendid chief at Payawan also wore many of these jewels, but his were of gold. Mr. Worcester distributed his white slips to the ever-eager multitudes, listened to reports, and held council with the head men; the people were fed with rice and meat, appeared thoroughly to enjoy themselves, and so the time passed.

The next morning, May 4th, we rode off. Shortly after leaving, we came suddenly upon a party apparently wrangling over a piece of meat, at a point where the trail was crossed by a small stream, flowing in a thin sheet over a smooth face of rock, twenty or more feet high, and tilted at about seventy degrees. The wranglers took alarm on our approach and scattered in all directions. One of them, a boy of perhaps sixteen, ran up the rock just described at full speed on his toes, and disappeared in the bushes at the top. Even if he had wished to use his hands, there was nothing to lay hold on. If I had not seen it performed with my own eyes, I should have declared the feat impossible: I mention it to mark the agility and strength of these people. Bear in mind that this youngster ran up, that the rock was not far from the vertical, and that the water-worn face was smooth and slippery. The thing was simply amazing.

We stopped again at our rest-house of the day before, meeting a few *cabecillas*, who showed us, with much pride, long ebony canes with silver tops, and inscriptions showing that they had been given by the Spanish Sovereign as rewards for faithful service, etc. One of these canes had been given by Maria Cristina. Others produced, from bamboo tubes, parchments of equally royal origin, setting forth in grandiloquent Spanish the confidence reposed by the Sovereign in such and such a *cabecilla*.

This day's journey was without incident of any sort. But, like all our other rides, it took us through country that beggars one's powers of description. We rode part of the way through an open forest, many of whose trees were of great height. One of these had, on a single large branch thrust out from the trunk at a height of sixty feet or so, as many bird's-nest ferns as could crowd upon it, looking comically like a row of hens roosting for the night. From the ground, about fifteen feet from the root of this same tree, rose a single-stem liana, joining the main trunk at the branch just mentioned; to this liana a huge bird-nest fern had attached itself twenty feet or more above the ground, completely surrounding the stem, a singular sight.

The day was fine, the trail good - like all the others of Gallman's trails, - and the people glad to see us. From time to time, as we neared Sabig, we were met by detachments, each with *gansas* and spears and our flag, and, besides, *bubud* in bamboo tubes; for, as must now be clear, the Ifugaos are a hospitable and courteous people, and we were made welcome wherever we went.

At about three we reached Sabig, situated on a hog-back between the trail on the left and a deep valley on the right. Here the people had built us the finest rest-house seen on the trip. For this house had separate rooms all opening on the same front, the roof being continued over the front so as to form a sort of veranda, under which a bamboo table had been set up. But, as though this were not enough, there were hanging-baskets of plants, bamboo and other leaves ornamenting the posts. Our cattle were as well off as we, having a real stable with separate stalls. Just north of the house, where the ground sloped, a platform had been excavated for dancing, which went on all night. There was the customary distribution of slips and the usual business of reports and interviews with the head men. Here we first saw the rice-terraces for which these mountain people are justly famous, that is, terraces climbing the mountain-side. But of weapons we saw none.

CHAPTER XVI

Change in aspect of country. - Mount Amuyao and the native legend of the flood. - Rice-terraces. - Banawe. - Mr. Worcester's first visit to this region. - Sports. - Absence of weapons. - Native arts and crafts.

We pushed on next morning early for Banawe, the capital of the sub-province of Ifugao, and Gallman's headquarters. The cheers of our late hosts accompanied us as we entered the trail and began to climb. The country now took on a different aspect, due to our increasing altitude. The valleys were sharper and narrower, and so of the peaks. From time to time we could see the proud crest of Amuyao ahead of us. Over 8,000 feet high, this mountain, whose name means "father of all peaks," or "father of mountains," is the Ararat of the Ifugaos. Their legend has it that, a flood overcoming the land, a father and five sons took refuge on this topmost peak, coming down with the waters as they fell. They even have their Cain, for one of these five was killed by a brother. This family traditionally are the ancestors of all the mountain people.

It took us some five hours to ride to Banawe, through a country of imposing beauty. It was not that we were in the presence of mighty ranges or peaks, so much as that the alternation of elevation with depression offered a bewildering variety of aspect. At every turn, turns as unnumbered this day as the woes of Greece, the

Cornelis De Witt Willcox

landscape changed its face. No sooner had one's appreciation become oriented, than it had to give way to the necessity of a fresh orientation. Of course there must be some orographic system; but to mark it, we should have had to fly over the land. To us on the trail it was not evident, mountain shouldering mountain, and valley swallowing valley, in confusion. And wherever possible, rice-terraces! If we posit the struggle for existence, then in this view alone these Ifugaos, and other highlanders as well, are a gallant people. Not every hillside will grow rice; if the soil be good, water will be lacking; or else, having water, the soil is poor. But, wherever the two conditions are combined, there will one find the slope terraced to the top, and scientifically terraced, too, so that every drop of water shall do its duty from top-side to bottom-side. The labor of original construction, always severe, in some cases must have been enormous, as we shall see later. Many of these terraces are hundreds of years old; their maintenance has required and continues to require constant watchfulness. Nearly every year the supply of rice runs short and the people fall back on *camotes* (sweet potatoes). And yet, in marked contrast with their cousins of the plains, whom these conditions would drive to helpless despair, we heard on this trip not one word of complaint. Not once did they put up a poor mouth and beg the Government to come to their help. On the contrary, they were cheerful throughout, knowing though they did that before the year was over they would probably all have to pull their gee-strings in a little tighter. It is not too much, therefore, to say that these highlanders are in a true sense a gallant people. Indeed, they are the best people of the Archipelago, and with any sort of chance they will prove it. This chance our Government, thanks to Mr. Worcester's initiative and sustained interest, is giving them, the first and only one they ever have had.

This digression brings us a little nearer to Banawe; we leave the terraced hills behind us, after noting how free of all plants the retaining-walls are kept, the sole exception here and there being the dongola, with its brilliant leaf of lustrous scarlet.

In time we began to descend, and finally there burst on the view the sharpest valley yet, as though some Almighty Power had split the mountains apart with a titanic ax. Down one flank we went with Banawe near the head, but farther off than we thought, because the trail was now filled with men that had come out to welcome us, all of whom insisted on shaking hands with all the *apos*. Our last three miles were a triumphal procession - columns, *gansas, bubud*, spears, shouts, escorts, flags. Every now and then a halt; a bamboo filled with *bubud* would be handed up, and everybody had to take a pull. Once I noticed Gallman in front hastily return the bamboo, and reach desperately for his water-bottle; the next man did the same thing. It was now my turn, and I understood; I tipped up the tube, and thought for the moment that I had filled my mouth with liquid fire, so hot was the stuff! If there had ever been any rice in the original composition, it had completely lost its identity in the fearful excess of pepper that characterized this particular vintage. It was hours and hours before our throats forgave us.

But at last we threaded our way down, and, turning sharp to the right, rode out on the small plateau that is Banawe, to be saluted and escorted by the Constabulary Guard and to be received by the shouts of thousands. They at once opened on us with speeches, but these were markedly fewer here than farther south.

The quarters of the Constabulary officers were hospitably put at our disposition, and our first enjoyment of them was the splendid shower.

Banawe stands at the head of a very deep valley, shut in by mountains on three sides; the stream sweeping the base of the plateau breaks through on the south. This plateau rises sharply from the floor of the valley; in fact, it is a tongue thrust out by the neighboring mountain, and forms a position of great natural strength against any enemy unprovided with firearms. Across the stream on the east mount the rice-terraces over a thousand feet above the level of the stream; a stupendous piece of work, surpassed at only one or two other places in Luzon. Elsewhere we saw terraces higher up, but none on so great a scale, so completely enlacing the slope from base to crest. The retaining walls here are all of stone, brought up by hand from the stream below. This stream makes its way down to the Mayoyao country, and I was told that the entire valley, thirty-five or forty miles, was a continuity of terraces. Indeed, it requires some time and reflection to realize how splendid this piece of work is: it is almost overwhelming to think what these people have done to get their daily bread. In contemplation of their successful labors, one is justified in believing that, if given a chance, they will yet count, and that heavily, in the destinies of the Archipelago.

Banawe was first visited by Mr. Worcester in 1903, coming down from the north with a party of Igorots. At the head of the pass he was met by an armed deputation of Ifugaos, who came to inquire the purpose of his visit. Was it peace or was it war? He could have either! But he must decide, and immediately. Assured as to the nature of the visit, the head man then gave

Mr. Worcester a white rooster, symbol of peace and amity, and escorted him in. But the accompanying Igorots came very near undoing all of Mr. Worcester's plans. Not only were they shut in during their stay, an obvious and necessary condition of good order and the preservation of peace, but, on Mr. Worcester's asking food for them, they were told they could have *camotes*, but no rice; that rice was the food of men and warriors, and *camotes* that of women and children, and that the Igorots were not men. This almost upset the apple-cart, for the Igorots in a rage at once demanded to be released from their confinement so as to show these Ifugaos who were the real men. But counsels of peace prevailed. In fact, it is a matter of astonishment that Mr. Worcester should be alive to-day, so great at the outset was the danger of personal communication with the wild men of Luzon. [30] It was not always a handsome white rooster, in token of peace, that was handed him; sometimes spears were thrown instead. However, on this trip of ours he got a whole poultry-yard of chickens, besides eggs in every stage of development from new-laid to that in which one could almost feel the pin-feathers sticking through the shell.

We spent two days here, and over 10,000 people were collected; some of them apparently showed traces of Japanese blood. Gallman allowed me to make an inspection of his Constabulary, their quarters and hospital. The men were as fine and as well set-up as those we saw at Kiangan. Everything was in immaculate condition, and ready for service. From the circumstance of this inspection, I could not afterward pass near the *cuartel* that the guard was not turned out for "the General" - a fact amusing to me, but which I carefully concealed from the other members of the party. During these two days, nights too, the *gansas* never stopped, neither did the dancing. Mr. Worcester distributed thousands of paper slips, and, besides, much serious business was dispatched. Then we had sports and ceremonial formal dances, much like those we saw at Kiangan, but better done. There was the same slow advance with shields, the same sacrifice of a pig - only this one was not speared, but had his insides mixed with a stick. He proved obstinate, however, and refused to die, so a man sat down on the ground, put his thumbs on the victim's throat, and choked him to death. Before that the usual lances had been laid across his body, and some *bubud* poured (judiciously, not extravagantly) on him as a libation. This was a head-dance, the taken head being simulated by a ball of fern-tree pith stuck on a spear fixed in the ground.

But these formal dances were not the only ones. Everybody danced, even Cootes and I again; but it was our last time. People kept on arriving from miles around, columns in single file, headed by men bearing *bubud*-jars on their heads. Every party, of course, brought its *gansas*, and had to give an exhibition of dancing on the parade. The arrival of the Mayoyao people on the 6th really made a picture, because we could see the trail for a long distance, occupied by men and women in single file, headed by Mr. Dorsey, of the Constabulary, on his pony. What with the *budbud*-bearers, the bright blue skirts of the women (color affected by these *rancherias*), and the cadence of the *gansas* to which they marched, it was a good sight, received with cheers. [31]

In general, but few parties were armed; and, as elsewhere, there were no old women. Some of the shyer people, coming from afar, had brought their spears, and, squatted on the slopes round about, apparently passed their time in silent contemplation of the great game going on below. Everybody seemed to be in a good humor. This was especially manifest in the great wrestling-match that took place on the afternoon of the 6th, when *rancheria* after *rancheria* sent up its best man to compete for the heads of the carabaos that had furnished meat for the multitude. The wrestling itself was excellent. The hold is taken with both hands on the gee-string in the small of the back; and, as all these men have strong and powerful legs, the events were hotly contested and never completed without a desperate struggle. Defeat was invariably accepted in a good spirit. As before remarked, however, when Mr. Worcester first organized these meetings, the *rancherias* came together armed to the teeth. Each would stick its spears in the ground, with shields leaning on them, and then wait for developments. Suspicion, hostility, defiance were the rule, and hostile collisions were more than once only narrowly averted. But on these occasions the native Constabulary proved its worth, by circulating in the crowd, separating parties, and so asserting the authority of the Government in favor of good order. Moreover, the highlanders soon learned to respect the power of "the spear that shoots six times" (the Krag magazine rifle, with which our Constabulary is armed); but it can not be repeated too often that our hold on these people is due almost entirely to the moral agencies we have employed.

Gradually Mr. Worcester satisfied some *rancherias*, at least, that had been open enemies for generations, whose men, in Mr. Worcester's graphic expression, had never seen one another except over the tops of their shields, that nothing was to be gained in the long run by this secular warfare; and his purpose in bringing the clans together is to make them know one another on peaceful terms, to show them that if rivalry exists, it can find a vent in wrestling, racing, throwing the spear, in sports generally. And they take naturally to sports, these highlanders. Success has crowned Mr. Worcester's efforts; in witness whereof this very concourse of Banawe may be cited, where over 10,000 persons, mostly unarmed, mingled freely with one another without so much as a brawl to disturb the peace.

Two years ago people would not go to Mayoyao from Banawe, through their own country, save in armed groups of ten to twelve; now women go alone in safety. And it is a significant fact that the Ifugaos are increasing in numbers. Of course, this particular subprovince is fortunate in having as its governor a man of Gallman's stamp. But it is generally true that village warfare is decreasing, and that travel between villages is increasing. These Ifugaos ten years ago had the reputation, and deserved it, of being the fiercest headhunters of Luzon. Gallman has tamed them so that today they have abandoned the taking of heads. Now what has been done with them can be done with others.

At Banawe we saw more examples of native arts and crafts than we had heretofore. For example, the pipe is smoked, and we saw some curious specimens in brass, much decorated with pendent chains; others were of wood, some double-bowled on the same stem. Some of the men wore helmets, or skull-caps, cut out of a single piece of wood. Other carved objects were statuettes, sitting and standing; these are *anitos*, frequently buried in the rice-paddies to make the crop good; besides, there were wooden spoons with human figures for handles, the bowls being symmetrical and well finished. Then there were rice-bowls, double and single, some of them stained black and varnished. Excellent baskets were seen, so solidly and strongly made of *bejuco* as to be well-nigh indestructible under ordinary conditions. Mr. Maimban got me a pair of defensive spears (so-called because never thrown, but used at close quarters) with hollow-ground blades of tempered steel, the head of the shaft being wrapped with *bejuco*, ornamentally stained and put on in geometrical patterns.

Our officials regarded this great meeting as entirely satisfactory. We made ready for an early start the next morning, saying good-bye to Browne, who had accompanied us from Bayombong, and who had shown me personally many courtesies. His last act of kindness was to take back with him the various things I had got together, and later to send them on to me at Manila. Our column was to be increased by a party of Ifugaos, whom, with a head man named Comhit, Gallman wished to take through the Bontok into the Kalinga country. The fact that these men returned safely unaccompanied by Gallman or any other American is the best possible proof of the positive results already achieved by our Government in civilizing the highlanders.

CHAPTER XVII

We ride to Bontok. - Bat-nets. - Character of the country. - Ambawan. - Difficulties of the trail. - Bird-scarers. - Talubin. - Bishop Carroll of Vigau. - We reach Bontok. - "The Star-Spangled Banner." - Appearance of the Bontok Igorot. - Incidents.

From Banawe we rode to Bontok, thirty-five miles, in one day, May 7th. This day it rained, the only rain we had during the whole trip, although the season was now on. But the disturbance in question was due to a typhoon far to the southward; and as it passed off into the China Sea, so did the day finally clear. Our first business this morning was to cross the pass on Polis Mountain, some 6,400 feet above sea-level, the highest elevation we reached. As we rode out of Banawe we could see on the wooded sky-line to our right front a cut as though of a road through the forest; it was not a road, of course, but an opening normal to the crest of the ridge. Across this a net is stretched, and the bats, flying in swarms by night to clear the top, drop into the cut on reaching it, and so are caught in the net in flying across. We saw several such bat-traps during our trip. In this way these highlanders eke out their meager supply of meat. The bat in question is not the animal we are familiar with, but the immensely larger fruit bat, the flesh of which is readily eaten. Our trail took us up, and sharply; by nine o'clock we had crowned the pass, and stopped for chow and rest. In front of us, as we looked back, plunged the deepest, sharpest valley yet seen, around the head of which we had ridden and across which we could look down on the Ifugao country we had just come from; down one side and up the other could be traced the remains of the old Spanish trail, a miracle of stupidity. To the right (west), but out of sight, lay Sapao, where the rice-terraces have received their greatest development, rising from the valley we were gazing into some 3,000 feet up the slope. Sapao, too, is the seat of the Ifugao steel industry, so that for many reasons I was sorry it was off our itinerary. The point where we were resting has some interest from its associations, for our troops reached it in their pursuit of Aguinaldo, at the end of a long day of rain, and had to spend the night without food or fire or sleep. It was not possible to light a pipe even, a *noche triste* indeed. Most of the men stood up all night, this being better than lying down in the mud; to march on was impossible, as the country was then trailless, except for the Spanish trail mentioned, to attempt which by night would have been suicide. A tropical forest can be pretty dreary in bad weather, almost as dreary as a Florida cypress swamp on a rainy Sunday.

We now made on, having crossed into Bontok sub-province, and by midday had reached a point on the trail above an Igorot village called Ambawan. Here we were met by a number of the officials of the province, who gave us a sumptuous tiffin in the rest-house. And here, too, we bought a number of baskets made in Ambawan, graceful of design and well-woven, though small. Governor Evans offered an escort of Constabulary through the next village, Talubin, the temper of its inhabitants being uncertain, but Mr. Forbes declined it, and ordered the escort sent back. We were riding as men of peace, determined to mark our confidence in the good intentions and behavior of the various *rancherias* we passed through.

Immediately on leaving Ambawan, we had to drop from the new trail (ours) to the old Spanish one for a short distance, for our trail had run plump upon a rock, waiting before removal for a little money to buy dynamite with. Having turned the rock, the climb back to the new trail proved to be quite a serious affair, as such things go, the path being so steep and so filled with loose sand and gravel clattering down the slope at each step that only one man leading his horse was allowed on it at a time, the next man not starting till his predecessor was well clear at the top. A loss of footing meant a tumble to the bottom, a matter of concern if we had all been on the path together. But finally we all got up and moved on, this time over the narrowest trail yet seen, a good part of the way not more than eighteen or twenty inches wide, with a smooth, bare slope of sixty to eighty degrees on the drop side, and the bottom of the valley one thousand to fifteen hundred feet or more below us. Many of us dismounted and walked, leading our horses for miles. With us went an Igorot guide or policeman, who carried a spear in one hand, and, although naked, held an umbrella over his head with the other, and a civilized umbrella too, no native thing. However, it must be admitted that it was raining.

The mists prevented any general view of the country; as a matter of fact, we were at such an elevation as to be riding in the clouds, which had come down by reason of the rain. However, the valleys below us were occasionally in plain enough sight, showing some cultivation here and there, rice and *camotes*, the latter occasionally in queer spiral beds. The bird-scarers, too, were ingenious: a board hung by a cord from another cord stretched between two long and highly flexible bamboos on opposite banks of a stream, would be carried down by the current until the tension of its cord became greater than the thrust of the stream, when it would fly back and thus cause the bamboo poles to shake. This motion was repeated without end, and communicated by other cords suitably attached to other bamboo poles set here and there in the adjacent rice-paddy. From these hung rough representations of birds, and a system was thus provided in a state of continious agitation over the area, frequently of many acres, to be protected. The idea is simple and efficacious.

This long stretch terminated in a land-slide leading down into the dry, rocky bed of a mountain stream. At the head of the slide we turned our mounts loose, and all got down as best we could, except Mr. Forbes, who rode down in state on his cow-pony. Once over, we crossed a village along the edge of a rice-terrace, in which our horses sank almost up to their knees. As the wall was fully fifteen feet high, a fall here into the paddy below would have been most serious; it would have been almost impossible to get one's horse out. However, all things come to an end; we crossed the stream below by a bridge, one at a time (for the bridge was uncertain), and found ourselves in Talubin, where we were warmly greeted by Bishop Carroll of Vigan and some of his priests. The Bishop, who was making the rounds of his diocese, had only a few days before fallen off the very trail we had just come over, and rolled down, pony and all, nearly two hundred feet, a lucky bush catching him before he had gone the remaining fourteen hundred or fifteen hundred.

Talubin somehow bears a poor reputation ; its

inhabitants have a villainous look, owing, no doubt, in part to their being as black and dirty as coal-heavers. This in turn is due to the habit of sleeping in closed huts without a single exit for the smoke of the fire these people invariably make at night, their cook-fire probably, for they cook in their huts. However this may be, the people of this *rancheria* showed neither pleasure nor curiosity on seeing us, and I noticed that a Constabulary guard was present, patrolling up and down, as it were, with bayonets fixed and never taking their eyes off the natives that appeared. These Igorots lacked the cheerfulness and openness of our recent friends, the Ifugaos. Their houses were not so good, built on the ground itself, and soot-black inside. The whole village was dirty and gloomy and depressing, and yet it stands on the bank of a clean, cheerful stream. However, the inevitable *gansas* were here, but silent; one of them tied by its string to a human jaw-bone as a handle. This, it seems, is the fashionable and correct way to carry a *gansa*. At Talubin the sun came out, and so did some bottles of excellent red wine which the Bishop and his priests were kind enough to give us. But we did not tarry long, for Bontok was still some miles away. So we said good-bye to the Bishop and his staff and continued on our way. The country changed its aspect on leaving Talubin: the hills are lower and more rounded, and many pines appeared. The trail was decidedly better, but turned and twisted right and left, up and down. The country began to take on an air of civilization - why not? We were nearing the provincial capital; some paddies and fields were even fenced. At last, it being now nearly five of the afternoon, we struck a longish descent; at its foot was a broad stream, on the other side of which we could see Bontok, with apparently the whole of its population gathered on the bank to receive us. And so it was: the grown-ups farther back, with marshalled throngs of children on the margin itself. As we drew near, these began to sing; while fording, the strains sounded familiar, and for cause: as we emerged, the "Star-Spangled Banner" burst full upon us, the shock being somewhat tempered by the *gansas* we could hear a little ahead. We rode past, got in, and went to our several quarters, Gallman and I to Governor Evans's cool and comfortable bungalow.

I took advantage of the remaining hour or so of daylight to get a general view of things. One's first impression of the Bontok Igorot is that he is violent and turbulent; it is perhaps more correct to say that, as compared with the Ifugao, he lacks discipline. It is certain that he is taller, without being stronger or more active or better built; in fact, as one goes north, the tribes increase in height and in wildness. The women share in the qualities noted. Both men and women were all over the place, and much vigorous dancing was going on. Using the same *gansa* as the Ifugao, the Igorot beats it on the convex side with a regular padded drumstick, whereas the Ifugao uses any casual stick on the concave side. Moreover, the Bontok dancers went around their circle, beating their *gansas* the while, in a sort of lope, the step being vigorous, long, easy, and high; as in all the other dances seen, the motion was against the sun. The *gansa* beat seemed to be at uniform intervals, all full notes. While our friends the Ifugaos were, on the whole, a quiet lot, these Bontok people seemed to be fond of making a noise, of shouting, of loud laughter. They appeared to be continually moving about, back and forth, restlessly and rapidly as though excited. On the whole, the impression produced by these people was not particularly agreeable; you felt that, while you might like the Banawe, you would always be on your guard against the Bontok. But it must be recollected that we had no such opportunity to see these people as we enjoyed in the case of Banawe and Andangle. The occasion was more exciting; they were more on show. It is not maintained that these are characteristics, simply that they appeared to be this afternoon and, indeed, during the remainder of our stay.

Individuals appeared to be friendly enough, though these were chiefly the older men. One of them, a total stranger to me, came up and intimated very clearly that he would like the transfer of the cigar I was smoking from my lips to his. In a case like this, it is certainly more blessed to give than to receive, but in spite of this Scriptural view of the matter, I nevertheless naturally hesitated to be the party of even the second part in a liberty of such magnitude, and on such short acquaintance, too. However I gave him the cigar; he received it with graciousness. I found now that I must give cigars to all the rest standing about, and, after emptying my pockets, sent for two boxes. An expectant crowd had in the meantime collected below, for we were standing on the upper veranda of Government House, and, on the two hundred cigars being thrown out to them all at one time, came together at the point of fall in the mightiest rush and crush of human beings I ever saw in my life. A foot-ball scrimmage under the old rules was nothing to it. Very few cigars came out unscathed, but the scramble was perfectly good-humored.

Of weapons there was almost none visible, no shields or spears, but here and there a head-ax. The usual fashion in clothes prevailed; gee-string for the men, and short sarong-like skirt for the women. Hair was worn long, many men gathering it up into a tiny brimless hat, for all the world like Tommy Atkins's pill-box, only worn squarely on the apex of the skull, and held on by a string passed through the hair in front. In this hat the pipe and tobacco are frequently carried. Many of these hats are beautifully made, and decorated; straw, dyed of various colors, being combined in geometrical patterns. Ordinary ones can be easily got; but, if ornamented with beads or shell, they command very high prices, one hundred and fifty pesos or more. Many men were elaborately tattooed, the pattern starting well down the chest on each side and running up around the front of the shoulder and part way down the arm. If, as is said, this elaborate tattoo indicates that its owner has killed a human being, then Bontok during our stay was full of men that had proved their valor in this particular way. Earrings were very common in both sexes; frequently the lobe was distended by a plug of wood, with no appreciable effect of ornament, and sometimes even torn open. In that case the earring would be held on by a string over the ear. One man came by with three earrings in the upper cartilage of each ear, one above the other. Still another had actually succeeded in persuading nature to form a socket of gristle just in front of each ear, the socket being in relief and carrying a bunch of feathers. A few men had even painted their faces scarlet or yellow. No one seemed to know the significance of this habit (commoner farther north than at Bontok), but the paint was put on much after the fashion prevailing in Manchuria, and, if possibly for the same reason, certainly with the same result. The pigment or color comes from a wild berry.

Cornelis De Witt Willcox

CHAPTER XVIII

Importance of Bontok. - Head-taking. - Atonement for bloodshed. - Sports. - Slapping game.

Bontok is a place of importance, as becomes the capital of the Mountain Province. Here are schools, both secular and religious; two churches in building (1910), one of stone (Protestant Episcopal), the other of brick (Roman Catholic), each with its priest in residence; a Constabulary headquarters; a brick-kiln, worked by Bontoks; a two-storied brick house, serving temporarily as Government House, club and assembly; a fine provincial Government House in building; streets laid off and some built up, these in the civilized town. This list is not to be smiled at; a beginning has been made, a good strong beginning, full of hope, if the unseen elements established and forces developed are given a fair chance. The place was important before we came in; the native part is ancient and has a municipal organization of some interest. Spain first occupied the place in 1855 and garrisoned it with several hundred Hokanos and Tagalogs. She has left behind a bad name; but the *insurrectos* (Aguinaldo's people), who drove the Spaniards out, have left a worse. Both took without paying, both robbed and killed; the *insurrectos* added lying.

Some four hundred Igorot warriors were persuaded by the *insurrectos* to join in resisting the Americans and went as far south as Caloocan just north of Manila, where, armed only with spears, axes, and shields, they took their place in line of battle, only to run when fire was opened. According to their own story, [32] which they relate with a good deal of humor, they never stopped until they reached their native heath, feeling that the *insurrectos* had played a trick on them. Accordingly, it is not surprising that when March went through Bontok after Aguinaldo, the Igorot should have befriended him, nor later that the way should have been easy for us when we came in to stay, about seven or eight years ago.

The site is attractive, a circular dish-shaped valley, about a mile and a half in diameter, bisected by the Rio [33] Chico de Cagayan, with mountains forming a scarp all around. Bontok stands on the left bank, and Samoki [34] on the right; separated only by a river easily fordable in the dry season, these two Igorot centers manage to live in tolerable peace with each other, but both have been steadily hostile to Talubin, only two hours away. However, it can not be too often said that this sort of hostility is diminishing, and perceptibly.

We spent two days at Bontok very quietly and agreeably. The first day, the 8th, was Sunday, and somehow or other I got to church (Father Clapp's, the Protestant Episcopal missionary's) only in time to see through the open door an Igorot boy, stark naked save gee-string and a little open coat, passing the plate. Father Clapp has been here seven years, has compiled a Bontok-English Dictionary, and translated the Gospel of Saint Mark into the vernacular. As already said, he has a school, a sort of hospital; is building a stone church; is full of his work, and deserves the warmest support. It must be very hard to get at what is going on behind the eyes of his native parishioners. For example, shortly before our arrival, a young Igorot had been confirmed by Bishop Brent. Now this boy was attending school, and in the school was another boy from a *rancheria* that had taken a head from the *rancheria* of the recent convert. When the latter's people learned of this, they sent for their boy, the recent convert, the Monday after confirmation, held a *canao* (killing a pig, dancing, and so on), and sent him back resolved to take vengeance by killing the boy from the offending *rancheria*. Accordingly, on Thursday, at night, the victim-to-be was lured behind the school-house under the pretext of getting a piece of meat, and, while his attention was held by an accomplice with the meat, the avenger came up behind, killed him, and was about to take his head when people came up and arrested him. This case illustrates the difficulties to be met in civilizing these people. Legally, under our view, this boy was a murderer; under his own customs and traditions, he had done a commendable thing. When the boys' school was first opened, they used to take their spears and shields into the room with them; this proving not only troublesome, but dangerous, their arms are now taken away from them every morning, and returned after school closes.

Many people came to see Governor Evans this day, among them a young man begging for the release of a prisoner held for murder. He really could not see why the man should not be set free, and sat patiently for two hours on his haunches, every now and then holding up and presenting a white rooster, which he was offering in exchange. The matter was not one for discussion at all, but Evans was as patient as his visitor, paying no attention to him whatever. Whenever the pleader could catch Evans's eye, up would go the rooster and be appealingly held out. Only two or three weeks before, a private of Constabulary had shot and killed the head man of Tinglayan some miles north of Bontok. He was arrested, of course, and when we came through was awaiting trial. But a deputation had come in to wait on Mr. Forbes, and ask for the slayer, so that they might kill him in turn, with proper ceremonies. Naturally the request was refused; but these people could not understand why, and went off in a state of sullen discontent. Here, again, was a conflict between our laws, the application of which we are bound to uphold, and native customs, having the force of law and so far regarded by the highlanders as meeting all necessities. The practice of head-hunting still exists in the Bontok country, though the steady discouragement of the Government is beginning to tell. Here in Bontok itself, a boy, employed as a servant in the Constabulary mess, dared not leave the mess quarters at night; in fact, was forbidden to. For his father, having a grudge against a man in Samoki across the river, had sent a party over to kill him. By some mistake, the wrong man was killed, and it was perfectly well understood in Bontok that the family of the victim were going to take the son's head in revenge, and were only waiting to catch him out before doing it. These homicides can, however, be atoned without further bloodshed, if the parties interested will agree to it. A more or less amusing instance in kind was recently furnished by the village of Basao, which had in the most unprovoked manner killed a citizen of a neighboring *rancheria*, the name of which I have unfortunately forgotten. The injured village at once made a *reclama* (*i.e.*, *reclamation*, claim for compensatory damages), and Basao agreed, the villages meeting to discuss the matter. When the claim was presented, Basao, to the unspeakable astonishment and indignation of the offended village, at once admitted the justice of the *reclama*, and handed over the damages - to-wit, one chicken and pesos six (three dollars). This was an insult to the claimant; for on these occasions it seems that each party takes advantage of the opportunity to tell the other what cowards they are, what thieves and liars, how poor and miserable they are, that they live on *camotes* - in short, to recite all the crimes and misdemeanors they have been guilty of from a time whereof the memory of man runneth not to the contrary, this recital being accompanied, of course, by an account of their own virtues, qualities, and wealth. The claimants in this case accordingly withdrew, held a consultation, and, returning, declared that in consequence of the insult put upon them the damages would have to be increased, and demanded one peso more! The body is always returned, and the damages cited are for a body accompanied by its head; if the head be lacking, the damages go up, no less than two hundred pesos, a fabulous sum in the mountains.

The highlanders [35] believe in bird signs and omens drawn from animals generally. A party sent out to arrest a criminal had been ordered to cross the river at a designated point. Returning without their man, the chief was asked where they had crossed, and, on answering at so-and-so (a different point from the one ordered), was asked why he had disobeyed orders. It seems that a crow had flown along the bank a little way, and, flying over, had alighted in a tree and looked fixedly at the party. This was enough: they simply had to cross at this point. Sent out again the next day, a snake wriggled across the trail, whereupon the chief exclaimed joyfully that he knew now they would get their man at such a spot and by one o'clock, that the snake showed this must happen. Unfortunately it did so happen!

The afternoon passed listening to stories and incidents like those just given, until it was time to go and see the sports. [36] These, with one exception, presented no peculiarity, races, jumping, tug-of-war, and a wheel-barrow race by young women, most of whom tried to escape when they learned what was in store for them. But the crowd laid hold on them and the event came off; the first heat culminating in a helpless mix-up, not ten yards from the starting-line, which was just what the crowd wanted and expected. The exception mentioned was notable, being a native game, played by two grown men. One of these sits on a box or bench and, putting his right heel on it, with both hands draws the skin on the outside of his right thigh tight and waits. The other man, standing behind the first, with a round-arm blow and open hand slaps the tightened part of the thigh of the man on the box, the point being to draw the blood up under the skin. The blow delivered, an umpire inspects, the American doctor officiating this afternoon, and, if the tiny drops appear, a prize is given. If no blood shows, the men change places, and the performance is repeated. The greatest interest was taken in the performance this afternoon, many pairs appearing to take and give the blow. The thing is not so easy as it looks, the umpire frequently shaking has head to show that no blood had been drawn. The prizes consisted of matches, which these highlanders are most eager to get.

The day closed with a *baile*, given by the Ilokanos living in Bontok. Many of these are leaving their narrow coastal plains on the shores of the China Sea and making their way through the passes to the interior, some of them going as far as the Cagayan country. It is only a question of time when they will have spread over the whole of Northern Luzon. This *baile* was like all native balls, *rigodon*, waltzes, and two-steps; remarkably well done too, these, considering that the *senoritas* wear the native slipper, the *chinela*, which is nothing more or less than a heelless bed-room slipper. But one *senorita* danced the *jota* for us, a graceful and charming dance, with one cavalier as her partner, friend or enemy according to the phase intended to be depicted.

CHAPTER XIX

The native village. - Houses. - Pitapit. - Native institutions. - Lumawig.

The next day, the 9th, Father Clapp very kindly offered to show Strong and me the native village, an invitation we made haste to accept. This village, if village it be, marches with the Christian town, so that we at once got into it, to find it a collection of huts put down higgledy-piggledy, with almost no reference to convenience of access. Streets, of course, there were none, nor even regular paths from house to house; you just picked your way from one habitation to the next as best you could, carefully avoiding the pig-sty which each considerable hut seemed to have. I wish I could say that the Igorot out of rude materials had built a simple but clean and commodious house! He has done nothing of the sort: his materials are rude enough, but his hut is small, low, black, and dirty, so far as one could tell in walking through. The poorer houses have two rooms, an inner and an outer, both very small (say 6 x 6 feet and 4 x 6 feet respectively, inside measurement), cooking being done in the outer and the inner serving as a sleeping-room. There is no flooring; although the fire is under the roof (grass thatch), no smoke-hole has been thought of, and as there are no window-openings, and the entrance is shut up tight by night and the fire kept up if the weather be cold, the interior is as black as one would expect from the

Cornelis De Witt Willcox

constant deposit of soot. The ridge-pole of the poorer houses is so low that a man of even small stature could not stand up under it. The well-to-do have better houses, not only larger, but having a sort of second story; these are soot-black, too. We made no examination of these, not even a cursory one. The pig-sty is usually next to the house, and is nothing but a rock-lined pit, open to the sky, except where the house is built directly over it.

It is astonishing that these people should not have evolved a better house, seeing that the Ifugaos have done it, and the Kalinga houses, which we were to see in a day or two, are really superior affairs.

Passing by a certain house, Father Clapp stopped and said, "Here is where Pitapit was born," and stood expectant. Strong and I looked furtively at each other; it was evident that we were supposed to know who Pitapit was. But as we did not, the question was put: "Who is Pitapit?" Father Clapp, gazing pityingly upon us, as though we had asked who George Washington was, then enlightened us. Pitapit is a Bontok boy of great natural qualities, so great, indeed, that he was sent to the States to a church school, where he had recently won a Greek prize in competition! Father Clapp was naturally very proud of this, as he well might be. The fact of the matter is that Igorot children are undeniably bright; given the chance, they will accomplish something. And I repeat what I have said before: we are trying to give them and their people a chance, the only one they have ever had.

We remarked, as we walked about this morning, that although Father Clapp seemed to know some of the people we met and would speak to them, they never returned his greeting. None of these highlanders have any words or custom of salutation. In the Ifugao country, however, they shake hands, and would frequently smile when on meeting them we would say, "*Mapud!*" - *i.e.*, "Good!" - the nearest thing to a greeting that our very scanty stock of Ifugao words afforded. But the Igorot never shook hands with us nor offered to: they have no smile for the stranger, though they seem good-humored enough among themselves.

Poor as we found the village on the material side, it has nevertheless some interesting institutional features. For example, it has sixteen wards, or *atos*, and each *ato* has its meeting-place, consisting of a circle of small boulders, where the men assemble to discuss matters affecting the *ato*, such as war and peace; for the *ato* is the political unit, and not the village as a whole. A remarkable thing is the family life, or lack of it rather: as soon as children are three or four years old, they leave the roof under which they were born and go to sleep, the boys in a sort of dormitory called *pabajunan*, occupied as well by the unmarried men, [37] and the girls in one called *olog*. And, as one may ask whether pearls are costly because ladies like them or whether ladies like pearls because they are costly, so here: Is the Igorot house so poor an affair because of the *olog*, etc., or does the *olog* exist because the house is poor? Be this as it may, and to resume, the children go on sleeping in their respective *pabajunan* and *olog* until they are grown up and married. A sort of trial marriage seems to exist; the young men freely visit the *olog* - indeed, are expected to. If results follow, it is a marriage, and the couple go to housekeeping; other-wise all the parties in interest are free. Marriage ties are respected, adultery being punished with death; but a man may have more than one wife, though usually

Cornelis De Witt Willcox

that number is not exceeded. However, a man was pointed out to us, who maintains in his desire for issue, but without avail, a regular harem, having no fewer than fifteen wives in different villages, he being a rich man.

Among other things shown us by Father Clapp was a circle of highly polished boulders, said traditionally to be the foundation of the house of Lumawig, the Deity of the Bontok. One stone was pierced by a round hole, made by Lumawig's spear: on arriving, he decided he would remain permanently in Bontok, and began by sticking the shaft of his spear in the stone in question - a very minor example, by the way, of his magical powers. More interesting, perhaps, than the ruins of Lumawig's house was a sacred grove on a hill rising just back of the village, in which, according to Father Clapp, certain rites and ceremonies are held once a year. The matter is one for experts, but it appears strange that this people should have a sacred grove, as being unusual.

We wound up our stay in Bontok by going to a grand dinner in Government House, given by Pack. [38]

CHAPTER XX

We push on north. - Banana skirts. - Albino child. - Pine uplands. - Glorious view.

Our two days' stay had greatly refreshed our horses and ponies, and they needed it, not only because of the work already done, but because of the effort we were going to ask of them during the next forty-eight hours, when the sum total of our ascents was to be 18,000 feet, and of descents the same, and the distance to be travelled seventy miles.

We continued our journey on the 10th, leaving Van Schaick behind, and also Cootes, both of whom had been taken ill, not seriously, but enough to make it safer to fall out than to go on. On this day, the relations between neighboring *rancherias* being uncertain, we changed *cargadoros* at the outskirts of each village we came to. We could undoubtedly have taken the same set of men through, but it was thought best not to try it. At the same time, the mere fact of our riding through unmolested, and still more the fact that Gallman was taking a party of Ifugaos with him to show them the country, is proof positive that peace is making its way in the North, just as it has already done farther south.

Our first day the going was very hilly, and very hot; we dismounted frequently so as to spare our cattle over the steepest ups and downs. As before, not only was

Cornelis De Witt Willcox

the scenery that unfolded itself, as we rose from the valley of the Rio Chico, of great beauty, but it increased in beauty the farther north we travelled. And I can not but regret again my inability to give some idea, however faint, of these mountains and valleys and rivers, especially of those that paraded themselves before us on the second day's ride.

About four hours out (the hour, and not the mile, being the unit of the highlands), as we were nearing the top of a ridge, a party of young women and girls came out of the wood on our left, each with a banana-leaf skirt on, no less and no more. They had simply stripped off one side of the leaf, and, after splitting the other into ribbons, had wrapped the stem about their waists, and there they were, each with a sufficient skirt. One of them had apparently never seen a horse before, and showed so much interest that Pack gallantly offered to let her mount his and take a ride. When the remainder of her party understood from her motions that she was actually going to bestride that monster, they set up a chorus of ear-piercing shrieks and screams and laid hold on their insane sister, and besought her with lamentations not to risk her life. During the struggle, Mr. Worcester came up and produced a diversion by offering red cloth, and, moving to the top of the ridge for the distribution, we found there some twenty-five or thirty more damsels, of all ages from grandmother to mere tot, and all banana-skirted. Mr. Worcester said that in all his experience he had never seen the like before. Heiser, in the meantime, had got out his camera and tried to form a group with the children in front and the older ones back. But when they realized that the effect of this would be to conceal all but the heads and shoulders of those in rear, the group broke up almost automatically, giving way to a line with arms linked, which no amount of effort on anyone's part succeeded in breaking. Each one was resolved to be in the picture at full length! In the crowd, looking on, was a man carrying an albino, a child two or three years of age, with absolutely fair white skin and yellow hair. It was sound asleep, and so I did not see its eyes, but otherwise it was a perfect albino; even here at home and as a normal child it would have been regarded as unusually fair. The pack had now got up, and Mr. Worcester began his issue. At his feet stood a little lassie, whom he overlooked, and whose countenance, as she saw the red cloth diminishing and likewise her chances, displayed the most vivid play of emotion. Finally, when the last yard of the stuff had been given out and she had got none of it, two large tears formed and ran down her cheeks. Poor little thing, but ten minutes ago she had braved it with the best of them, but her skirt had now suddenly gone out of style! The eternal feminine! I neither saw nor heard any other child cry during the whole trip. As we rode off, our banana-grove accompanied us part way, singing, and, disappearing behind a hillock on our left,

"Unrobed and unabashed in Arcady,"
shifted from Nature's weave to man's.

From this point to the stream at its foot, the ridge on which we found ourselves was completely bare of trees, and presented a different appearance from any other so far seen or to be seen, tremendous rounded masses. One of these had been split through the middle by a recent earthquake: the right half, as we looked at it, dropping down eight or ten feet below the other, a splendid example of convulsive power. Across the stream and nearly at the top of the climb that followed we halted for chow and sleep under some tall pines.

Two hours later we were off again, through a country from which all visible suggestion of the tropics had disappeared. We were passing through red soil uplands, grass and pines, with a clear view in all directions.

Passing on, we now faced one of the most disagreeable ascents of the whole trip: a bare, mountainous hill facing south, so steep that we had to switch-back it to the top, with the sun blazing down on our backs, the hour being three of the afternoon, and not a breath of wind going. It was too steep to ride, and our water-bottles were empty. When we got to the top, Gallman and I, we could both have exclaimed with Villon,

"*Je crache blanc comme coton.*"

What wonder, then, that on finding a clear, cold spring at hand, Gallman should have drunk his fill of the cool water, and that he should have persuaded me, against my better judgment, to take a swallow of it, just one swallow, no more? Who would have believed that a mere taste of such innocent-looking, refreshing water could have had such dire consequences? For it made me ill for six weeks, at times all but disabling me. However, as water, it was irreproachable; and, anyway, as though to compensate the tiresome climb just finished, we had before us now one of the most glorious views imaginable. From far to the south - indeed, from the blue mountains bounding the view miles away, the silver ribbon of the Rio Chico unrolled itself in a straight line between green-sloped mountains, rising from its very banks and towering into the clouds. At our feet, but far below, the river turned square to the east in a boiling rapid between gigantic walls of rock, the mountains here yielding to its sweep in a broadening valley only to press on it beyond and thrust it back on its way northward. It was all splendid and simple; if you please, nothing but a stream filling the intersecting slopes of a wedge-shaped valley and turning off because it had to. But the serenity of the whole composition: gray rocks, shining waters, green slopes; white mists, enveloping the crests, smiling in the afternoon sun! Jaded as were our faculties of admiration by the many exquisite scenes we had already passed through, this one held us. We had to leave it, though, making our halt later for the night at a rest-house in a pine wood, near a good stream.

Cornelis De Witt Willcox

CHAPTER XXI

Deep valley. - A poor *rancheria*. - Escort of boys. - Descent of Tinglayan Hill. - Sullen reception at Tinglayan. - Bangad. - First view of the Kalingas. - Arrival at Lubuagan.

We were off early the next morning, the 11th, our destination being Lubuagan, the capital of the Kalinga country. We had a long, hard day before us. As I was about to mount, I noticed that Doyle, Mr. Forbes's groom, looked seedy, and learned that Bubud had broken loose in the night and gone the rounds of the herd, kicking every animal in it before he could be caught, and so robbing poor Doyle of a good part of his sleep. After riding a bit through the pines, the ground apparently dropped off in front of us out of sight, rising in a counter slope on the other side, in a great green wall from which sprang a hogback; only this time it was a razor-back, so sharp was its edge, up which back and forth ran the trail. It was another of those deep knife-like valleys; this one, however, challenging our passage, and justly, for it was more canon than valley, and it took us nearly two hours to cross it. But it was worth the trouble and time. For imagine a canon with forested sides and carpeted in green from the stream in its bed to the highest bounding ridge! Near the top we came upon a bank of pitcher-plants, the pitchers of some of them being fully six inches long. A mile or so farther on, we halted and dismounted near a little *rancheria*, Butbut by name, in a corner of the hills, the people of which had been assembled for the "Commission." These were the only physically degraded-looking people we saw on the trip; small of stature, feeble-looking and spiritless. The reason was not far to seek: it is probable that they live hungry, through lack of suitable ground for rice-cultivation, and because their neighbors are hostile. Now, I take it on myself to say that it is just this sort of thing that will come to an end if Mr. Worcester is allowed to carry out his policies. For, with free communication and diminishing hostility, interchange of commodities must needs take place. Indeed, the relations existing between *rancherias* are nothing but our own system of high protection carried to a logical extreme by imposing a prohibitive tariff on heads! Fundamentally, granted an extremely limited food-supply, every stranger is an enemy, and the shortest way to be rid of the difficulty involved in his presence is to reduce him to the impossibility of eating.

On reaching the top of Tinglayan Hill, which we did shortly after leaving the poor people just mentioned, we saw a man coming towards us accompanied by thirty or forty boys not more than ten or eleven years of age, all gee-stringed, and eight of them carrying head-axes on their hips. When the man got up, he handed Mr. Worcester a bamboo about a yard long. Mr. Worcester drank and then passed it on back to us, the best stuff, it seemed to us that hot morning, we had ever tasted. We were now in the *basi* country; this being a sort of fermented sugar-cane juice, judiciously diluted with water. [39] The boys now formed a sort of column with the ax-bearers immediately in front of Mr. Worcester as a guard of honor, and we got a good look at them, well-built, erect, of a light brown, with black flowing hair. They were as healthy-looking as possible, and, what is more, intelligent of countenance - by all odds the brightest, most cheerful lot of youngsters we had yet seen. As we moved off they set up a chant, clear and wild, beginning with a high note and concluding with as deep a one as their young voices could compass. The thing was as beautiful as it was wild, and astonishing from the number and range of notes used.

Marching thus, we came upon a large gathering of men, women, and children, to whom various gifts of cloth, pins, beads, etc., were made. Here Gallman found, to his amazement, that he could understand the speech of these people. Not trusting his own ear in the matter, he sent Comhit about to talk to them, and reported afterward that both not only had understood what was said, but had made their own selves understood. Neither of them could make out a word in the poor village we had just passed through, nor anywhere else on the road in the Bontok country.

We now began the long descent to Tinglayan, seven miles, most of us walking and leading our ponies. At Tinglayan, instead of the usual cheerful crowd waiting to welcome us, we found only a few extremely sullen men and women, who held themselves persistently aloof. There were no children, neither were chickens nor eggs offered - a bad sign. This reception was due entirely to the refusal of the authorities to give up the Constabulary private that had but recently shot and killed the head man of the *rancheria*, as already explained. However, in time, Mr. Worcester prevailed on the few present to accept gifts, and we affected not to notice the character of our reception, not only the best, but indeed the only thing to do. Here we had *chow.* We were now directly on the left bank of the Chico, and, passing on, found the country more open, and so better cultivated, the paddies being broad, the retaining-walls low, and the countryside generally wearing an air of peace and affluence. This impression deepened as we reached Bangad, extremely well situated on a tongue running out at right angles to the main course of hills. Here was a semblance of a street, following the trail, or, rather, the trail, going through, had followed the street. The houses were larger, cleaner, better built; in short, substantial. One of them, unfinished, gave us some idea of its construction: floor sills on posts to ground; roof frame of planks, 1 x 6 inches, bent over to form the sides of the house when completed, all hard wood, without a single nail, the whole being held together by mortises and tenons and other joints, accurately made and neatly fitted. We remained here an hour or so, while the "Commission" was making gifts to the people. No weapons whatever were visible, and the women and children moved about freely without a trace of shyness or fear. Our way beyond the village now took us by many turns back to the river, the trail finally rising in the side of a vertical cliff, such that by leaning over a little one could look past one's stirrup straight down to the water many hundreds of feet below. At the highest point the trail turned sharp to the left, almost back on itself. I am proud to say that I rode it all, but was thankful when it was behind us. Heiser's horse this day got three of his feet over the edge and rolled down eighty or ninety feet, Heiser having jumped off in time to let his mount go alone. It was fortunate for him that this particular cliff was not the scene of this fall. Some three miles farther, on fording a stream, we passed from Bontok into Kalinga, and were met by Mr. Hale, the Governor, with two warriors, tall and slender, broad of chest and thin of flank, with red and yellow gee-strings, tufts of brilliant feathers in their hair, and highly polished head-axes on their hips. Greetings over, we went on, and soon reached the river again, going down the left bank until we came upon what seemed to me to be a most interesting geological formation. For the bank of the river here rose sharply in a rounded, elongated mass, the end of which toward us was cut off, as it were, just as one cuts off the end of a loaf of bread, and showed alternate thin black and white strata only three or four inches thick tilted at an angle of sixty or seventy degrees and mounting several hundred feet in the air. The trail itself had been cut out in the side of the mass, and was so narrow that not only was everyone ordered to dismount, but the American horses were all unsaddled, the inch or two so gained being important in passing along. The black and white strata showing on the path, there was an opportunity to examine them; the black layers were so soft and friable that they could be gouged out with ease with the hand, and appeared to be vegetable, while the white stripes were most probably limestone. This bit of the trail is regarded as dangerous, because the rock overhead is continually breaking loose and tumbling down; for this reason it was unsafe to try to dislodge pieces for later examination. One of our *cargadores*, as it was, fell over, his pack getting knocked in, while he himself escaped with a bruise or two. It was a bad place! At the end of it a host of Kalingas acclaimed us, as picturesque as the warriors we had met at the stream, and took over the pack. Leaving the river, we began what appeared to be an interminable climb to Lubuagan. Up ran the trail, disappearing far ahead above us, behind the shoulder of the ridge; and we would all be hoping (those of us to whom the country was new) that Lubuagan would be just around the turn, only to find we had the same sort of climb to another shoulder; the fact being that the ridge here thrust itself out in rising echeloned spurs, each one of which had to be turned, so that we began to doubt if there was such a place as the capital of the Kalinga province. In truth, we had been up since 3:30 and were nearly spent from heat and thirst. But at last we made the final turn, and entered upon a narrow green valley, with a bold, clear stream rushing over and between the rocks that filled its bed. Broad-leafed plants nodded a welcome from the waters, as we rode through the grateful shadow of the overarching trees, and shining pools smiled upon us. We crossed a bridge, came down a bit, and, breaking through the fringe of trees and shrubs, saw before us the place-of-arms of Lubuagan.

CHAPTER XXII

Splendid appearance of the Kalingas. - Dancing. -
Lubuagan. - *Basi*. - Councils. - Bustles and braids. -
Jewels and weapons. - Excellent houses.

The sight that greeted us was stirring, suggesting to the
piously minded Bishop Heber's unmatched lines:

> "A noble army, men and boys,
> The matron and the maid."

There must have been thousands of people, as many
women as men, and almost as many children as
women, all of whom set up a mighty shout as our little
column emerged. But what especially and immediately
caught the eye was the brilliancy of the scene. For,
whereas the people so far encountered had impressed
us by the sobriety of color displayed, these Kalingas
blazed out upon us in the most vivid reds and yellows.
Many of them, women as well as men, had on tight-
fitting Moro jackets of red and yellow stripes; but
whatever it was - skirt, jacket, or gee-string - only one
pattern showed itself, the alternation of red and yellow,
well brought out by the clear brown of the skin. As
though this were not enough, some men had adorned
their abundant black hair with scarlet hibiscus flowers,
and all, or nearly all, wore plumes of feathers, one over
each ear. Each *rancheria* has its distinctive plume; as,
red with black tips, black with red, all red, white with

black, and so on, some with notched and others with natural edges. Many men had axes on their hips. The whole effect was startling, and all the more that these people, erect, sinewy, of excellent build like their comrades farther south, were perceptibly taller, men five feet ten inches tall not being uncommon. Add to this a stateliness of walk and carriage, combined with a natural, wholly unconscious ease and grace of motion, and it is easy to imagine the fine impression made upon us by our first look upon these assembled people. It is not too much to say that the whole sight was splendid; but, more than this, under the surface of things, it was easy to catch at once the possibility of a real development by these people under any sort of opportunity whatever.

We had hardly dismounted before the dancing began, in general against the sun, as elsewhere. Each *rancheria* of the many present had its dancers, and all made a display. One event, if the sporting term be permissible, seemed to be a sort of "follow-my-leader"; the motions, however, being confined to the circle, across which the file would go from time to time, thus differing from any other dance seen. In some cases, the step was bold and lively; in others, slow and stately, with arms outstretched. The *gansa* music was not nearly so well marked as that of the Ifugaos; it seemed to lack definition (an opinion advanced with some hesitation, and which a professional musician might not agree with). Sometimes women only appeared; in fact, up here the sexes did not mix in the dance. If we had remained longer in this part of the country, perhaps the differences and characteristics of this expression of native genius would have stood out more clearly; but in our short time, with so much dancing going on, impressions necessarily overlapped. And, in

Cornelis De Witt Willcox

any case, shortly after our arrival, night fell, putting an end to the show, and we betook ourselves to our quarters; Captain Harris, of the local Constabulary forces, most kindly receiving some of us in his house.

Kalinga is neither a race nor a tribe name, but a word meaning "enemy" or "outlaw," as though the hand of the people that bear it had been against everybody's else. These people have been great head-hunters, and have not yet entirely abandoned the practice, though it is steadily diminishing. It should be recollected, however, that it is only within the last three or four years that we have had any relations with them, Mr. Worcester's first visit to Lubuagan having occurred in 1907. On this occasion, immediately on arriving, he was shut up with his party in a house; and all night a lively debate went on outside as to whether the next morning his head should be taken or not, his native interpreter informing him of the progress of opinion as the night wore on.

In some respects these Kalingas differed from the tribes already visited. Their superior height has already been noted. It may be noted further that they are sloe-eyed, and their eyes are wide apart. It is said that they have an infusion of Moro blood, brought in, many years ago, by exiles from Moroland turned loose on the north coast of Luzon by the Spaniards, with the expectation that the local tribes would kill them; instead, they intermarried. Among themselves they call their important men *dato*, a Moro title, and their Moro dress has already been mentioned. They will not marry outside of their own blood, and their women, so we were told, would not look at a white man.

Lubuagan itself is extremely well situated on a gigantic

terrace-like slope, as though, as at Kiangan, an avalanche of earth had burst through the rim of encompassing mountains. Here live the Governor of the province and the inspector of Constabulary with a detachment; their houses, with the *cuartel* and public offices, are disposed around a sort of parade, divided into an upper and a lower terrace. Aguinaldo marched through the place during his flight, and left behind seventeen of his men, sick and wounded. He had no sooner gone than these were all taken out and beheaded. The native town lies above and just back of the parade, with its houses running well up on the slopes. These are, everywhere possible, terraced for rice, and so successfully that two crops are made every year, as against only one at Bontok and elsewhere. It follows that the Kalingas have more to eat than their relatives to the south, and that is perhaps one reason of their greater stature.

The morning of the 12th, our one full day at Lubuagan, broke clear, bright, and hot, and so the day remained. Events during the next few hours had no particular axis. We looked on mostly, though, of course, here as elsewhere, business there was to be dispatched. The upper terrace was the scene of crowded activity, being packed with people from sunrise to sunset. Dancing went on the whole day; the sound of the *gansa* never ceased. A particularly interesting dance was that of a number of little girls, eight or ten years of age, who went through their steps with the greatest seriousness and dignity, a very pretty sight. In yet another the performers, nine all told, grown men, attracted attention from the fact that the handles of their *gansas* were human lower jaws, apparently new, in the teeth of two of which gold fillings glistened. The Ifugaos, who, it will be recollected, had accompanied us from

Banawe, also danced, their steps, motions, and music forming a sharp contrast. This dance over, Comhit could not restrain himself, but made a speech, in which he declared that "These people up here, the Kalingas, are very good people indeed, but not so good as the Ifugaos." Fortunately, only his own people understood him. He had noticed on the way that the people we passed offered nothing to drink to the traveller, and had commented freely to Gallman on this lack of hospitality, so different from his country's habits. We had nothing to complain of, however, on this score at Lubuagan, for *basi* circulated freely the whole day, being passed along sometimes in a tin cup, at others in a bamboo; everybody drank out of one and the same vessel. On the whole, this *basi* was poor stuff, not nearly so good as *bubud*. Harris told me after the day was over, and we had taken innumerable tastes, at least, of the brew (for one must drink when it is passed), that in preparing *basi* a dog's heart, [40] cut up into bits, is added to the fermenting liquid to give it body. One man amused us by going around with a bamboo six inches or more in diameter and at least eight feet in length over his shoulder, and obligingly stopping to let his friends bend down the mouth and help themselves - a "long" drink if there ever was one!

But it was not all *basi* and dancing: councils were held, the visiting *rancherias* profiting by the opportunity of enforced peace to clear up issues. At these councils, which came off in the open, on the parade, the people of the *rancherias* interested would sit on the ground in a circle, maintaining absolute silence, while their spokesmen, a head man from each, walked around in the circle. The man who had the floor, so to say, would remain behind and address his adversary in the debate, who meantime kept on walking around with his back turned squarely on the speaker. As soon as the argument in hand had been made, both would counter-march, and the listener would now become the speaker. A great part of the debate was taken up on both sides by a recital of the crimes and misdemeanors of which the other party had been guilty. In one of these councils, one debater - wearing civilized dress, by the way - suddenly broke through the circle and disappeared, much to our astonishment, until it was explained that his opponent in the debate had charged him with having recently poisoned six persons; as this was perilously near the truth, the criminal simply ran away. The accuser was a fine-looking man, splendidly dressed, of a haughty countenance, displaying the greatest contempt for all the arguments addressed to him, his impatience being marked by "*Has!*" accompanied by stamping on the ground the while and striking it with the butt of his spear. This chief was in confinement at Lubuagan, but, to save his face, Governor Hale had enlarged him during our stay.

Naturally there was an opportunity during the day of observing many things in some detail. Who shall say, for example, that the Kalingas are not civilized? The women and girls all wear bustles, a continuous affair made of *bejuco*, an endless roll, in short, of varying radius, that over the small of the back being considerably the greatest. The top of the skirt is tucked in all round, instead of being directly on the skin, as farther south. In further proof of the local civilization, the women wear false hair. One matron was obliging enough to undo her coiffure for our benefit, and held out by its end, for our admiring inspection, a mighty wisp nearly three feet long. She put it back on for us after the manner, as I have since been informed, of a coronet braid. The men gave fewer evidences of civilization, unless smoking cigars in holders will serve. However, one man brought up his wife and children and regularly introduced them to us, the woman doing her part with great coolness, while the children gave every sign of terror. This incident struck me as being very unusual. Everyone had on at least one necklace, and some three or four necklaces, of dog-teeth, of agate beads (these being immensely prized, agate not being native to the Philippines), or of anything else the form, color, and hardness of which could make it answer for purposes of ornament. One young woman had on sleigh-bells, the tinkle of which we heard before we saw its source, an incongruous sound in those parts. These bells must have been brought down by Chinese trading from the plains of Manchuria. Two or three young men displayed what looked like lapis lazuli around their necks, but what turned out at closer quarters to be pieces of a blue china dinner-plate. They had cut out the white interior and then divided the rim radially, the jewels thus formed being all of the same size and shape, with perfectly smooth edges. Here, too, were the same pill-box hats as those seen at Bontok, some elaborately beaded and costing from one to five carabaos apiece; in one case the lid of a tomato tin had been pressed into service as a hat. But the finest thing of all was the head-ax, a beautiful and cruel-looking weapon, the head having on one side an edge curving back toward the shaft, and on the other a point. To keep the weapon from slipping out of the hand, a stud is left in the hard wood shaft, about two-thirds of the way from the head, the shaft itself being protected by a steel sheathing half way down; the remainder being ornamented with decorative brass plates and strips, and the end shod in a ferrule of silver. The top of the ax is not straight, but curved, both edge and point taking, as it were, their origin in this curve; the edge is formed by a double chamfer, the ax-blade being of uniform thickness. All together, this weapon is perhaps more original and characteristic than any other native to the Philippine Archipelago. With it goes the Kalinga shield of soft wood, made in one piece, with the usual three horns or projections at the top and two at the bottom. These projections, however, are cylindrical, and the outside ones are continued down the edge of the shield and so form ribs. In the ordinary Igorot shield the horns are flat, merely prolonging the surface of the shield, or else presenting only a very small relief. As usual, a lacing of *bejuco* across top and bottom protects the shield against a separation in the event of an unlucky stroke splitting it in two.

We found the town unusually clean. Public latrines exist, and public drinking-tanks, both put in by Governor Hale, and highly approved of the people. The houses themselves were the best we had seen, some of them hexagonal in ground plan, and built of hard woods. The pigs stay underneath, to be sure, but their place is kept clean. Rich men have rows of plates, the dinner-plates of civilization, all around their houses, and take-up floors of split bamboo are common, being rolled up and washed in the neighboring stream with commendable frequency. All together, Lubuagan made the impression of an affluent, not to say opulent, center, inhabited by a brave, proud, and self-respecting people.

CHAPTER XXIII

We leave the mountains. - Nanong. - Passage of the
Chico. - The Apayao. - Tabuk. - The party breaks up. -
Desolate plain. - The Cagayan Valley. - Enrile.

The morning of Friday, May 13th, broke clear after a
night of hard rain. We set off before sunrise, our way
now taking us eastward for the last stage of the
mountain journey proper. The whole earth this
morning seemed to be a-drip: every stream was
rushing, and banks of cloud, fog, and mist crowned the
heights and filled the valleys. To describe even
approximately our course as we descended from the
great terrace of Lubuagan is well-nigh impossible; but,
as we came down, scene after scene of the greatest
beauty offered itself to our admiration. The landscape
softened too; we were leaving the high mountain land
behind us, not too suddenly, however; for example, at
one point a huge valley lay below us, bounded on the
other side by a tremendous vertical wall of rock, over
which fell a powerful stream. I estimated the fall at the
time as at least four hundred feet.

In due course we came to an affluent of our old friend
the Chico, and had to ford. The stream was up, but we
got over without mishap. Fording is always a delicate
operation in these, mountains after a hard rain, since no
one can ever tell what the nature of the footing will be,
because of the boulders swept down. On this occasion

Evans's pony stopped short in mid-stream, refusing either to move on or back. There was nothing for it but dismount and investigate, Evans discovering that his pony had put one foot down between two large stones close together and so was simply caught fast. The country had now become decidedly more open; the trail for long stretches was almost a road. As a matter of fact, we were on the old main line of communication from the highlands to the Cagayan Valley. We made our first halt at Nanong, where everybody brought in gifts of chickens, eggs, and *camotes* and received beads, red cloth, pins and needles in return. What made a particular impression here was the number of children brought in, all wide-eyed, sloe-eyed, and some of them extremely pretty. The remainder of the day we spent going down the left bank of the Chico, encountered again at Nanong. Shortly after leaving this point two large monkeys, brown with white breasts, appeared on the edge of the trail, apparently protesting with the utmost indignation against our presence in those parts. Harris remarked that once passing this point alone he had run into eighteen of them, and that for a time he thought they were going to dispute his passage. These were the only animals we saw on the whole trip, not counting a few birds. The valley opened hereabouts, and on the other bank, the right, a sharp-edged terrace came into view, fully three hundred feet above the river and continuing for miles as far as the eye could see. This must be an unusually good example of river terrace. On our side the trail was cut out of the cliff, solid rock, with a straight drop to the river below, a stretch of two of the hottest miles conceivable, what with the full blaze of the sun and the heat radiated and reflected from the face of the cliff. I was so weak from the water I had drunk the other day that I dismounted and walked the whole way, so that, if knocked out by the heat, I should at least not fall off my pony; a tumble on the wrong side would have brought the journey to a very sudden end. But, fortunately, nothing happened, and we at last got down to the level of the river again, only to find it half in flood and fording out of the question. We were on the upstream side of a huge dome of rock, rising from the river itself, the only way around which was to cross twice. The rest of the party coming up with the *cargadores*, we had to wait until bamboo rafts could be built, the raft really being nothing but a flat bundle lashed together with *bejuco*. In this case our rafts were so small that under the weight of only one man and his kit they immediately became submarines, so that one got partially wet crossing. Our horses and ponies were swum over.

We were six hours making the two passages; still we were in luck, for had the stream been really up, we should simply have had to camp on its bank and wait for the waters to fall, a fate that sometimes overtakes the traveller in a country where an innocent stream may become a raging torrent almost while one is looking at it.

We slept that night in a rest-house just across the river from Tabuk, and next morning the party divided, Mr. Worcester, Dr. Strong, Governor Pack, and Lieutenant-Governor Villamor to continue the mountain trip into Apayao, while the remainder of us, having been invited to accompany Mr. Worcester only as far as Tabuk, went on to the Cagayan River. It may be of interest, however, to say a few words here about the Apayao country, my authority being the "Seventh Annual Report of the Secretary of the Interior to the Philippine Commission" for the fiscal year 1907-1908.

This country was first visited by Mr. Worcester in 1906. The Spanish Government never having succeeded in gaining a foothold in it. "During the insurrection Lieutenant Gilmore, of the United States Navy, and his fellow-captives were taken into the southern part of it and there abandoned." "So far as is known, no white man had ever penetrated the southern and central portions of Apayao until" Mr. Worcester, suitably accompanied and escorted, crossed the Cordillera, in 1906, from North Ilokos. A later expedition, commanded by a Constabulary officer, was attacked, not necessarily from any hostility to it as such, but because it was accompanied by natives hostile to a *rancheria* (Guenned) approached on the way. A punitive expedition, led by the same officer, afterward met with some success, but American popularity suffered in consequence. The Apayao country is the only sub-province under a native Governor, and its Governor, Senor Blas Villamor, is the only Filipino that has ever shown any interest in or sympathy for the highlanders. His task has been a difficult one; for example, his only line of communication, the Abulug River, runs through a territory inhabited by Negritos, who had been so abused by the Christian natives on the one hand, and whose heads had been so diligently sought by the wild Tinguians of the mountains, on the other, that they had acquired the habit of greeting strangers with poisoned arrows. His mountain region itself was inhabited by inveterate head-hunters, most of whom had never even seen a white man. Conditions are improving, however; the raids against the Christian and Negrito inhabitants of the lowlands of Cagayan have been completely checked, and Mr. Worcester hopes that head-hunting will diminish. It still exists. Strong told me, on his return to Manila, that, looking into a head-basket after leaving Tabuk, he found in it fresh fragments of a human skull; for the Apayaos take the skull like the other highlanders, but unlike them, break it into pieces. But with these people head-hunting is a part of their religious belief, and so all the harder to uproot. With the others it is a matter of vengeance, or else even of sport. "On the other hand, the people of Apayao have many good qualities. They are physically well-developed and are quite cleanly. They erect beautifully constructed houses. Their women are well clothed, and both men and women love handsome ornaments. They are quite industrious agriculturists and are now begging for seed and for domestic animals in order that they may emulate their Christian neighbors in the raising of agricultural products."

Of course we should have been very glad to go on with Mr. Worcester into the Apayao country if he had asked us; but it is practically trailless as yet, and for a party as large as ours would have been, questions of supply and transportation would have been difficult, to say nothing of the impolicy of taking a large number into the country at all. And so, on Saturday morning, May 14th, we shook hands with Mr. Worcester and his companions. His progress so far had been an unqualified success, unmarred by a single adverse incident, for the deplorable loss of life at Kiangan could in no wise be attributed to our presence or to the occasion. What the results of the visit of 1910 will be, only time can tell; but experience shows that every year marks an advance in the spread of friendly relations, not only between the Government and the people, but between the subdivisions of the people itself. [41]

The Chico being still up when we reached it, we crossed again on submarines, climbed the bank, and found ourselves in Tabuk (or Talbok), the most pestilential hole in the Archipelago. Nothing is left of it now but a ruinous church and one or two houses. The first mass was said here or hereabouts in 1689, by the Dominicans, who kept up the mission until the monks all died of fever. Did an occasional officer in the old days prove objectionable to the authorities in Manila, he got an order to proceed to Tabuk for station; it was almost certain that he would never return. The point is of unquestionable importance, commanding, as it does, the main outlet, of the Kalinga country to the plains of the Cagayan Valley; and so our own Government undertook to garrison it with Constabulary as a check on raids. The garrison remained long enough to be carried out on stretchers, and was removed to Lu-bagan, where the check is just as complete and personal control possible.

We had a long and hard day before us, but we did not know it when we set out from Tabuk at about seven in the morning. Gallman, Harris, and I kept together; our first business was to cross a vast, roughly circular plain fifteen miles in diameter, and densely overgrown with a rough, reedy grass two feet and more high. A footpath ran across the plain, visible for only a very short distance ahead as long as one was in it, but imperceptible twenty yards to the right or left. To lose this path would have been a serious matter, as it would have been a heart-breaking thing to force one's way through the undisturbed grass.

It would be hard to imagine anything else more wearisome than that fifteen-mile stretch. The sun was riding high in the heavens, "shining on both sides of the hill"; not a breath of wind was stirring nor was there, barring a rare bird or two, a sign of life save the thousands of flies which, as our ponies pushed aside the grass overhanging the path, rose in clouds only to settle on our faces, hands, necks, backs, everywhere. We began by brushing them off, but it was of no use, and so we rode with our faces turned to a dim haze of low mountains bounding the plain on the east, and themselves dominated by still another range, the Sierra Madre, so distant as to look like a bank of immovable blue cloud. For miles our plodding seemed to bring them no nearer. If we could only get out of that sea of olive-gray grass, on which the heavy, stifling air seemed to press, and reach those nearer mountains! Twice the path led us into sinks or depressions fully ninety or one hundred feet below the level of the plain; why these could not have been avoided when the path was first struck out is hard to imagine, unless it was to get to water. For one of these sinks boasted of a clear, bold stream with all of its course underground save the part in the depression. In both were full-grown trees and grateful shade. Had we not been pressed to get through, it would have been interesting to explore these huge sinks; but we passed on, the flies, which had abandoned us on our descent, rejoining us when we climbed out on the other side. In time we reached our mountains, arid, bare, eroded, wind-bitten, and made our way slowly and painfully up and through the pass, our trail hereabouts being nothing but a trench so deep and narrow that part of the way we could not keep our feet in the stirrups. As we neared the crest of the range the pass disappeared, and for the last half-mile or so we attacked the ridge directly. When we got to the top, we found a gallant breeze blowing, and, spreading out before us, the vast plains of the Cagayan Valley. Far over in the east, and apparently no nearer than ever, rose the blue, cloud-like mountains of the Sierra Madre, now showing like a wall, which indeed they are, and one which no man has so far succeeded in scaling. But not a sign of life, of man or beast, caught our eye. And yet this valley is an empire in itself; its axial stream, the Rio Grande de Cagayan, or Ibanag, the "Philippine Tagus" of the ancient chronicles, the longest river of the Archipelago, by overflowing its banks every year, renews the fertility of the soil wherever its waters can reach. We stood here on the ridge a long time, resting and looking. Below us green ribbons, following the undulations of the plain, marked the trail of various water-courses; but, apart from this evidence of Nature's living forces, somehow or other the entire landscape was silent and desolate. We now began the descent, leading our ponies, for it was too steep to ride, and at last came to a stream where we found shade and grass, and, better yet, the advance guard of the party with food and drink ready. Our next stage was over rolling country, covered with fine short grass; once over this, the ground broke in our front, and we made the descent, finally coming out on the lowest floor of the valley at Enrile, two or three miles from the river. Night was falling as we made our way through its grass-grown streets, finding the air heavy, the people dull-looking, and everything commonplace: we had already begun to miss our mountains.

CHAPTER XXIV

Tobacco industry. - Tuguegarao. - Caves. - The Cagayan River. - Barangayans. - Aparri. - Island of Fuga. - Sail for Manila. - Stop at Vigan. - Arrival at Manila.

The great valley in which we now found ourselves really deserves more notice than perhaps it is suitable to give it here. As everyone knows, it furnishes the best tobacco of the Islands, tobacco that under proper care would prove a dangerous rival to that of Cuba, though it can never quite equal the product of the Vuelta Abajo. The cattle industry should prosper here - in fact, did a few years ago; the broad savannas, some of which we had crossed, furnishing excellent pasturage. It was proved long ago that this region was naturally adapted to the culture of silk and to the raising of indigo and sugar-cane. While tobacco was a Government monopoly, [42] the valley was wealthy, traces of wealth being still found in the hands of the people under the form of jewels, some of them costly and beautiful.

The passage of the Payne bill has already brightened the prospects of the people, and especially of the small growers, for prices paid on the spot have already gone up very considerably. The valley is sure to flourish before many years shall have passed, and nothing else would so much hasten this end as the completion of the railway from Manila. But when we passed through, a sort of general apathy seemed to fill the air: the people were listless, and so much of the tobacco crop as we could see looked neglected. A partial explanation is to be found in the belief, wide-spread in these parts at this time, that the comet had come to mark the end of all things, and that any work done would be wasted. This belief, however, did not check the native and courteous hospitality of the people; all of us were taken in for the night, Evans and I going to Senor Cipriano Pagula-yan's, where we found an excellent dinner awaiting us - in particular, coffee of superlative excellence. Don Cipriano was very modest about it, explaining that the coffee had been roasted only after our arrival and ground just before it was set on; but none the less it was admirable. Now, this coffee, of course, was grown in the valley, and there is no reason why its cultivation should not be taken up on a large scale for export.

Enrile held us only for the night. The next morning we all mounted, alas! for the last time, and, escorted by a great number of local magnates, took the road for the river. Here we left our mounts to Doyle, who was to return with them to Baguio. It was with great regret that I parted from Bubud: he had carried me faithfully and well, and I shall not soon forget his saucy head, looking after us as we got down the bank to go on board the motor-launch of the Tabacalera. [43]

In a few minutes we had crossed and landed at Tuguegarao, the capital of the province, and still retaining traces of its wealth and importance in the great days of the tobacco monopoly. It has an imposing church built of brick, a hospital, and a Dominican college, all of substantial construction; its streets are broad and well laid out, but of the town itself not much can be said, as a fire swept off most of it a few years ago. Still Filipino towns rise easily from the ashes, and there is no reason why prosperity should not again smile upon this ancient borough.

We tarried two or three days in Tuguegarao, waiting for river transportation and meanwhile greatly enjoying the hospitality so generously shown us. Major Knauber, of the Constabulary, and Mr. Justice Campbell, of the Court of First Instance, invited me to stay with them in a fine old Spanish house they had together. Every evening Herr - , of the - Company, had us to dinner in his beautiful bungalow. At a grand *baile* given us the day after our arrival, Heiser asked me if I had not dined that day and the day before at Herr - 's; on my saying yes, he laughed and remarked that he had just taken up his cook as a leper to be sent to the leper hospital on the Island of Culion. But in the East nobody bothers about a thing like that.

Tuguegarao is a point of departure for some interesting trips, notably one to some limestone caves, larger than the Mammoth Cave of Kentucky. In one of these caves, receiving light, air, and moisture from fissures in the natural surface of the ground, palms (cocoa and other), bamboos, and other plants and trees are growing in natural miniature. I was told that this cave was fascinating and that I ought to go and see it. But time was pressing; although the commanding General had set no limit on my absence, I felt I ought now to return. Accordingly, on the morning of the 18th, our transportation being ready, Mr. Justice Campbell and I went aboard a motor-launch and set out for Aparri, at the mouth of the river.

All river trips here in the East have an interest; this one

proved no exception to the general rule, though it presented nothing especially worthy of record. But the Rio Grande is the great road of the Valley, to such an extent, indeed, that there are no land roads to speak of. We passed between low, muddy banks, frequently of uncertain disposition, as though wondering how much longer they could possibly resist the wash of the current. The stream itself is shallow, uncharted, unbeaconed; its navigation requires constant attention, which it certainly got this day from our quartermaster, who remained on duty for ten consecutive hours. We had the ill-luck not to see a single crocodile, although the river is said to be full of them, all of ferocious temper. On the other hand, we did see the oddest possible ferry: a bundle or raft of bamboo, with chairs on top, towed across stream by a carabao regularly hitched up to it and getting over himself by swimming. This he does on an even keel, his backbone being entirely out of the water when under way.

There is nothing picturesque about the lower reaches of the Rio Grande, though its upper course, through hilly country, is different in this respect. The remains of one or two old towns, cut in two by the shift of the river-bed, excited our curiosity. So did, from to time, the *barangayans*, or native river-boats, huge, clumsy, ill-built, and generally with but four or five inches of free-board amidships on full load. These craft look as though they ought to sink by mere capillary attraction. However, people are born, live, and die aboard of them, so they must be safe enough. In the afternoon the river widened and its right bank, anyway, grew bolder and occasionally more permanent-looking, and finally, about an hour before sunset, we perceived the low white godowns of Aparri. We landed not at a wharf, but at the outer edge of the huddle of craft crowding the water front, and put up at the Fonda de Aparri, having done eighty-odd miles in a little over ten hours.

All the tobacco of the Valley reaches the world through Aparri; it is consequently a port of considerable importance. But it has no safe anchorage and is frightfully exposed to typhoons, all of which, if they do not pass over the place directly, somehow or other appear to step aside to give this region a blow. There is a never-ending conflict in the adjacent waters between the currents of the China Sea and those of the Pacific, making navigation hazardous, and for small boats perilous. On the day of our arrival, calm and fair as it was, a tremendous surf was beating on the bar, the spray and foam mounting in a regular wall many feet high, and driven up, not by the gradual attack of an advancing wave, but by the tireless energy of angry waters ceaselessly beating upon the same spot.

Of Aparri itself little can be said here: but, small as it is, it has nevertheless the bustle of all seaports in activity. Many of its streets are paved with cobblestones, and some of its buildings are, if not handsome, at least substantial. But it is cursed with flies: in our inn, otherwise comfortable enough, the kitchen and the temple of Venus Cloacina were side by side. The flies were all the more annoying that we had seen none in the mountains, nor indeed do I recollect ever having seen them in any number elsewhere in the Archipelago than at Aparri and in the never-to-be-forgotten plain of Tabuk. However, we survived the flies, and late in the afternoon of the third day went on board a Spanish steamer bound for Manila. We used our cabin to stow our kit, but lived and slept on the deck of the poop, the main deck between which and the forecastle was crowded with natives. Poor things! Each family appeared to have an area assigned to it, on which were piled indiscriminately all its earthly possessions in the shape of clothes, bags, pots and pans generally; the heap once formed, its owners sat and slept on it, with the inevitable family rooster at its highest point lording it over all. In fact, every spot on the main deck not otherwise occupied was simply filled with roosters, all challenging one another night and day by indefatigable crowing. As illustrating the difficulties of navigation in these parts, our steamer was two hours getting out of the river and across the bar, a matter of not more than a mile. Once out, she began to roll and pitch in an incomprehensible manner, seeing there was no wind and no sea. It was simply the never-ending contest between the Pacific Ocean and the China Sea. Once fairly in the latter, she behaved steadily enough.

Our journey was without incident; it did not, much to my disappointment, include the side trip sometimes made to the Babuyanes Islands for cattle. One of these islands, Fuga, is especially interesting; urn-burial prevailed in it in the past, the urns in some cases being arranged in a circle around a central urn or altar. Moreover, there is in Fuga a stone building known as the "Castle," with arched doorways, said not to be of Spanish origin, and near by is a plain strewn with human skulls and other bones, probably the scene of a battle. The skulls are remarkable from their great size, some of them being reported as extraordinary in this respect. The present inhabitants of these islands and of the Batanes live in stone houses, much like those of North Ireland and the islands west of Scotland. [44] And so we had hoped, Campbell and I, that we might get at least a look at Fuga. For, although it lies near to Aparri, it is hard to reach; small boats, even on calm, smooth days, being occasionally caught in the wicked

Cornelis De Witt Willcox

currents of these waters and swamped out of hand. The next morning we made Kurrimao, which has a shoreline strikingly picturesque in a land almost surfeited with the picturesque. We stayed long enough to take on a number of carabaos, which were swum out to the ship, and then hauled out of the water by a sling passed around their horns.

Our next stop was at Vigan, a well-built town, many of whose houses are of stone. We reached the town in a motor-car, passing through well cultivated fields of maguey. The mountains, rising abruptly from the coastal plain, are here cut by the famous Abra de Vigan, a conspicuous gap serving as a land-mark to the mariner for miles. And it is the custom to take a ride of many hours up the pass, and then come down the rapids in two, on bamboo rafts built for the purpose. This is a most exciting trip; alas! we had to be contented with an account of it! But Vigan itself was worth the trouble of going ashore; its churches and monasteries are extensive, dignified of appearance, and far less dilapidated than is unfortunately so frequently the case elsewhere in the Islands. Not the least interesting item of our very short stay was a visit to a new house, built and owned by an Ilokano, and equipped with the most recent American plumbing. The house itself happily was after the old Spanish plan, the only one really suited to this climate and latitude. But then the Ilokanos are the most businesslike and thrifty of all the civilized inhabitants: their migration to other parts, a movement encouraged of long date by the Spanish authorities, is one of the most hopeful present-day signs of the Archipelago, I was sorry to take my leave of Vigan; the place and its environs seemed full of interest. One more stop we made at San Fernando de Union the following day, a clean-built town, but otherwise of no special characteristics. Here we met an officer of Constabulary that had been recently stationed at Lubuagan, who told us of coming suddenly one day upon a fight between two bodies of Kalingas, numbering twenty or twenty-five men each, and this in Lubuagan itself. According to our ideas, it was no fight at all, the champions of each side engaging in single combat, while the rest looked on and shouted, waiting their turn. One man had already been killed, his headless trunk lying on the ground. On the approach of the officer they all ran. Here, too, we heard from another Constabulary officer, that the *insurrectos* in 1898-1899 forced the Igorots to carry bells and other loot taken from the *conventos* and churches, and would shoot the *cargadores* if they stumbled or fell, or could go no farther under the weights they were carrying.

Twenty-four hours later we steamed up Manila Bay. The trip was over.

CHAPTER XXV

Future of the highlanders. - Origin of our effort to improve their condition. - Impolicy of any change in present administration. - Transfer of control of wild tribes to Christianized Filipinos. - Comparison of our course with that of the Japanese in Formosa.

The question now presents itself: What is to become of these highlanders of Northern Luzon? And if the answer to be given is here applied only to them, let it be distinctly understood that logically the question may be put in respect of all the wild people of the Philippines. Of these there are over one million in a total population of perhaps eight millions. At once it appears that any conclusions we may draw, any speculations we may cherish, in respect of the Archipelago, as being inhabited by a Christian people unjustly deprived of liberty by us, must be subject to a very large and important correction. Limiting our inquiry to Luzon alone, let it be recollected that of its 4,000,000 population nearly four hundred thousand, or one-tenth, are highlanders, and that these highlanders, in all probability, arrived in the Islands at an earlier date than their Christianized cousins of the lowlands. Let us recollect further that these people are ethnologically not savages at all; not only are they workers in steel and wood, weavers of cloth, but hydraulic agriculturists of the very highest merit. On the side of moral qualities they invite our approving attention: they speak the truth, they look one straight in the eye, they are hospitable, courageous, and uncomplaining; their women are on a footing of equality, more or less, with the men, and are respected by them. Where they have had an opportunity, they have shown an aptitude to learn of no mean quality. Physically they are the best people of the Archipelago, and under this head would be remarkable anywhere else in the world. Now, the Spaniards, with a few exceptions, made no systematic, continuous attempt to civilize these peoples; or, if they did, no measurable results have come down to our own day, even Villaverde's efforts, genuine as they were, having left almost no trace. So far from having done anything for the hillmen, the record of the Spanish at the very few points garrisoned by them is one of injustice and robbery, and worse. That of the Filipinos, [45] in imitation of their Spanish masters, is no better. At any rate, when we took over the Archipelago in 1898, a vast area of Luzon was held by a people who looked, and justly, so far as their experience had gone, upon the white man and his Filipino understudy as an enemy. The difficulty of guiding and controlling these people undoubtedly had been (and still is) great, and partly accounts for the state of affairs we encountered when we first entered the country, but it was necessarily no greater for our predecessors in the Islands than it has been for us. Now, where they failed, we, it may be said without fear of contradiction, are succeeding, and it is but the simplest act of justice to say that the credit for our success belongs to the Secretary of the Interior of the Philippine Islands, Mr. Dean C. Worcester. He would be the last man on earth to say that his success is complete; on the contrary, he would assert that a very great quantity of work yet remains to be done, and that what he has done so far is but the beginning. But it is nevertheless a successful beginning, and successful because it rests on the solid foundation of honesty and fair dealing, and is inspired by interest in and sympathy for a vast body of people universally hated and feared by the Filipino, and until lately neglected and misunderstood by almost everybody else.

The physical difficulty alone of reaching these various peoples was not only very great, but mere presence in their country involved great risk of one's life. Again, the absence of even the rudest form of tribal organization made the way hard. Take the Ifugaos, for example, about 120,000 in number, all speaking essentially the same language, inhabiting the same country, and having the same origins and traditions. Yet this large body was and is yet broken up into separate *rancherias*, or settlements, each formerly hostile to all the others, this hostility being so great that merely to walk into a neighboring *rancheria* in plain sight, not more than two miles off across the valley, was a sure way to commit suicide. And what is true of the Ifugaos is true of all the others. Could any other field have been more unpromising, have offered more difficulties? There were those thousands of savages shut up in their all but inaccessible mountains. Why not leave them there, to take one another's heads when occasion offered? They raised nothing but rice and sweet potatoes, anyway, and not enough of those to keep from going hungry. Why concern one's self about them, when there was already so much to be done elsewhere?

To Mr. Worcester's everlasting honor, be it said, he took no such view. On the contrary, he went to work, and that after a simple fashion, but then, all great things are simple! The first thing was to see the people himself; and then came the beginning of the solution, to push practicable roads and trails through the country. Once these established, communication and interchange would follow, and the way would be cleared for the betterment of relations and the removal of misunderstandings. Today an American may ride through the country alone, unarmed and unmolested; [46] twenty years ago a Spaniard trying the same thing would have lost his head within the first five miles. And this difference is fundamentally due to the fact, already mentioned, of the honesty of our relations with these simple mountaineers. We have their confidence and their esteem and their respect, and this in spite of the necessity under which our authorities have constantly labored of punishing them when necessary and of insisting upon law and order wherever our jurisdiction prevails. The lesson has been hard to learn, but it has been driven home. The truth of the matter is, that a great missionary work has been begun; missionary not in the limited sense of forcing upon the understanding of a yet circumscribed people a religion unintelligible to them, but in the sense of teaching peace and harmony, respect for order, obedience to law, regard for the rights of others.

A beginning accordingly has been made, but what is to be the end? We should not stay for an answer, could we but feel sure that but one answer were possible. But we can not feel sure on this head; the people of the Islands, whether civilized or uncivilized, have not yet gone far enough to proceed alone. To drop the work now, nay, to lessen it, would merely be inviting a return to former evil conditions. No greater disaster could befall these highlanders to-day than a change entailing a diminution of the interest and sympathy felt for them at the seat of government. It is best to be plain about this matter: the Filipinos of the lowlands dislike the highlander as much as they fear and dread him. They apparently can not bear the idea that but three or four hundred years ago they too were barbarians; [47] for this reason the consideration of the highlander is distasteful and offensive to them. The appropriations of the Philippine Assembly for the necessary administration of the Mountain Province are none too great; they would cease entirely could the Assembly have its own way in the matter. The system of communications, so well begun and already so productive of happy results, would come to an end. To turn the destiny of the highlander over to the lowlander is, figuratively speaking, simply to write his sentence of death; to condemn as fair a land as the sun shines on to renewed barbarism. We are shut up to this conclusion, not by theoretical considerations, but by experience. The matter is worth examining a little closely, covering, as it does, not only the hill tribes, but non-Christians everywhere else.

Certain persons have demanded from time to time that the control of non-Christian tribes shall be turned over to the Filipinos. Now, pointing out in passing that the Filipinos and the non-Christians are distinct peoples, fully as distinct as the Dutch and the Germans, and that the Filipinos have no just claim to the ownership of the territory occupied by the wild men, let us ask ourselves if the Filipinos are able and fit to control the non-Christian tribes. [48]

Consider for a moment the facts set out in the following extracts:

"With rare exceptions, the Filipinos are profoundly ignorant of the wild men and their ways. They seem to have failed to grasp the fact that the non-Christians, who have been contemptuously referred to in the Filipino press as a 'few thousand savages asking only to be let alone,' number approximately a million and constitute a full eighth of the population of the Archipelago."

"The average hillman hates the Filipinos on account of the abuses which his people have suffered at their hands, and despises them because of their inferior physical development and their comparatively peaceful disposition, while the average Filipino who has ever come in close contact with wild men despises them on account of their low social development, and, in the case of the more warlike tribes, fears them because of their past record for taking sudden and bloody vengeance for real or fancied wrongs."

"It is impossible to avoid plain speaking if this question is to be intelligently discussed; and the hard fact is, that wherever the Filipinos have come in close contact with the non-Christian inhabitants, the latter have almost invariably suffered at their hands grave wrongs, which the more warlike tribes, at least, have been quick to avenge. Thus a wall of prejudice and hatred has been built up between the Filipinos and the non-Christian tribes. It is a noteworthy fact that hostile feeling toward the Filipinos is strong even among people like the Tinguians who, barring their religious beliefs, are in many ways as highly civilized as are their Ilocano neighbors,"

"The success of American rule over the non-Christian tribes of the Philippines is chiefly due to the friendly feeling which has been brought about."

"The wild man has now learned for the first time that he has rights entitled to a respect other than that which he can enforce with his lance and his head-axe. He has found justice in the courts. His property and his life have been made safe, and the American governor, who punishes him sternly when he kills, is his friend and protector so long as he behaves himself."

"Finally, it should be clearly borne in mind that the Filipinos have been given an excellent opportunity to demonstrate practically their interest in the non-Christians, and their ability wisely to direct the affairs of primitive peoples. While the inhabitants of the Mountain Province, Nueva Vizcaya, Agusan, and the Moro Province are not now subject to control by them, and the inhabitants of Mindoro and Palawan are subject to their control only through the Philippine Legislature, there are non-Christian inhabitants in the provinces of Cagayan, Isabela [and eighteen others].

"At the outset, these governors and provincial boards [*i.e.*, of the provinces just mentioned] exercised over their non-Christian constitutents precisely the same control they had over Filipinos. To the best of my knowledge and belief, not one single important measure looking to the betterment of the condition of these non-Christian inhabitants was ever inaugurated by a Filipino during this period. Indeed, the fact that no expense would be voluntarily incurred for them became so evident as to render necessary the passage, on December 16, 1905, of an act setting aside a portion of the public revenues for the exclusive benefit of the non-Christians.

"After Apayao was established as a sub-province of Cagayan and the duty of providing funds for the maintenance of its government was explicitly imposed upon the provincial board of that province, the governor stated to me that, in his opinion, it would be useless to make the necessary expenditure, and that, in his opinion, it would be better to kill all the savages in Apayao! As they number some 52,000, this method of settling their affairs would have been open to practical difficulties, apart from any humanitarian consideration!"

"Contrast with this record of inaction and lack of interest the record of the special Government provinces [49] and the Moro Province, where dwell really formidable tribes, which have until recently engaged in piracy, head-hunting, and murder. Here very extensive lines of communication have been opened up by the building of roads and trails and the clearing of rivers. A good state of public order has been established. Head-hunting, slavery, and piracy are now very rare. The liquor traffic has been almost completely suppressed. Life and property have been rendered comparatively safe, and in much of the territory entirely so. In many instances, the wild men are being successfully used to police their own country. Agriculture is being developed. Unspeakably filthy towns have been made clean and sanitary. The people are learning to abandon human sacrifices and animal sacrifices and to come to the doctor when injured or ill. Numerous schools have been established and are in successful operation. The old sharply drawn tribal lines are disappearing. Bontoc Igorots, Ifugaos, and Kalingas now visit each other's territory. At the same time that all of this has been accomplished, the good-will of the people themselves has been secured. They are outspoken in their appreciation of what has been done for them and in their expression of the wish that

American rule should continue. They would be horror-stricken at the thought of being turned over to Filipino control," [50]

"So far as concerns the warlike tribes, the work for their advancement thus far accomplished would promptly be lost; for they would instantly offer armed resistance to Filipino control, and the old haphazard intermittent warfare, profitless and worse than profitless for both peoples, would be resumed."

"I say, in all kindness, but with deep conviction, that there is no reason for believing that Filipino control of the more pacific non-Christian tribes would not promptly result in the re-establishment of the old system of oppression which Americans have found it necessary to combat from the day when military rule was first established in these islands until now. I speak whereof I know when I say that the people of these tribes have been warned, over and over again, by those interested in re-establishing the old regime, that American control in the Philippines will be only temporary, and that when the government is turned over to the Filipinos the tribesmen will be punished for their present 'insubordination' and failure tamely to submit to injustice and oppression, as many of them formerly did."

These extracts speak for themselves. So far as is known, the report from which they are drawn has gone unchallenged. Is it necessary any further to consider the question of a transfer of control from the present authorities to the Filipinos or to any other authority? Would not any change in the present administration be singularly unwise? Of course, the views and arguments set forth here are extremely unpopular among the politicians of the native ruling class. But then no Filipino likes the plain, unvarnished truth, a fact that should receive full weight in considering any demand or request of native or racial origin, involving questions of government.

With our own treatment of the American Indian in mind, our people should be the last to consent to any change in the relations or administration of the wild men of the Philippine Islands not fully justified by the amplest necessity, not warranted by well-grounded hopes of greater improvement. These men, for the first time in their history, are having a chance. That chance is fair to-day, and will continue fair so long as its administration lies in American hands., competent, trained, and experienced.

In taking over the Philippines, we have incidentally become responsible for a large number of wild men. Their fate is bound up in that of the Islands. Now, these islands may remain under our control, or they may not. Obviously, then, the question has its political side: we may grant full international independence to the Philippines. In the belief of some this would be merely a signal for civil war in the Archipelago, the issue of which no man can guess. But whether or not, in granting independence to the Philippines, we shall be signing the death-warrant of the highlander. Let us repeat that, this people form one-tenth of the population of Luzon: save as we arc helping him, he can not as yet assert himself beyond the reach of his spear. Shall we be the ones to mark this as the limit beyond which he shall never go? Let us not deceive ourselves: a grant of independence means the abandonment of hundreds of thousands of people to perpetual barbarism.

What would happen if the Islands fell into alien hands of course no one can tell. But there is strong ground for believing that Japan would enter a mighty bid for the sovereignty of the Archipelago, if we ever contemplate parting with it. Now, Japan in Formosa has for years been struggling, and without success, to control or subdue the aborigines of the mountains, a people of the same blood as the Igorots, of the same habits and traits, savage head-hunters, the terror of all the plainsmen of no matter what origin. It is interesting to read [51] that "among other measures taken by the Japanese authorities to 'control' the aborigines was the erection of barbed wire entanglements charged with electricity," the idea being, after surrounding a savage position by these entanglements, to have the troops drive the savages upon them. Many people have refused to believe that this electrical process has ever been put into effect, but the Kobe newspaper goes on to quote the correspondent of the *Times* in confirmation. And a correspondent from Shanghai, writing [52] to give the truth about the state of affairs in Formosa and to defend the Japanese against the charge of ill-treating the savages, nevertheless admits having been shown the entanglements, which, he says, are "as harmless as any ordinary fence wire during the day, except in cases of serious uprising on the part of the savages. At night it is charged, but all the savages know this grave fact." According to the *Times* correspondent, some three hundred miles have already been set up, and the work will be pushed until the aborigines "are wholly caged." Lastly, the *Chronicle* reports the Governor-General of Formosa as fixing a term of three years for the suppression of the bravest and fiercest tribe of all, numbering 50,000, at a cost of 17,000,000 yen. Now, we have no interest here or elsewhere in what is, after all, a municipal affair of Japan's. She must and will settle her own problems as seems best to her, and, if she is driven to "suppress" her Formosan aborigines, it is none of our business. Moreover, before pronouncing upon the matter, we should in all fairness hear the other side, although it does look as though the electric wire fence must be admitted. But there is enough in what is reported from Formosa to give us pause when we consider the possibility of parting with the control of the Philippine Islands, whether to Japan or to any other nation.

In so far as the wild tribes of the Archipelago are concerned, we have made a happy beginning; we owe it to our self-respect to carry on the work to a happy end. This we can do by heeding the simplest of rules: Leave well alone.

THE INDEPENDENCE OF THE PHILIPPINES.

"Am I my brother's keeper?" *Genesis iv. 9.*

"If we lose sight of the welfare of the people in a creed or a phrase or a doctrine, we have taken leave of our intelligence, and we have proved ourselves unfit for leadership." - *A Letter to Uncle Sam.*

Shall we give their independence to the Philippines? To this question an answer is still to be made by the American people. Not only do we not know whether we shall give this independence or not, but we have not yet decided whether we ought to or not. Even if we could suppose that the country had made up its mind on the subject, it would still be true that no competent authority has considered the manner in which our country would translate its desires into action, whether in one direction or another.

The reason of this state of affairs is not far to seek: our people neither know anything about these islands, nor do they care anything about them. Perhaps it is more accurate to say that our ignorance is the logical result of our indifference. The Islands are far away, as it were, inhabited by a different race, busied, on the whole, about things that form no part of our life, whether national or private. We have, as a people, bestowed no serious thought upon them; we have not yet raised the disposition to be made of them to the dignity of a national question.

Cornelis De Witt Willcox

SECTION I

I.

The Philippines became ours by the fortune of war. On the subsidence of the immediate questions raised by the war, we have continued in the ownership of the Islands without concerning ourselves thus far as to the ultimate place they are to occupy in our national ecomony. Of this state of affairs, but one opinion can be expressed: it is extraordinary. Even in a grossly material point of view, our attitude is indefensible; if we regard ourselves as landlords, we are indifferent to our tenants; if as mere owners, then are we careless of the future of our property. We have not assumed the responsibilities involved with any national sense of responsibility; we have neither declared nor formed any policy. But in this fact lies the extraordinariness of the situation. Of the soundness of our title to the Islands at international law there is not the shadow of a doubt; the Islands are ours. What do we intend to do with them? Why have we not, after fourteen years' possession, found an answer to the question, or, in other words, declared a policy? Nations, no less than individuals, must take an interest in their property, and society demands as a right that any property of whatever nature shall be adjusted in respect of relations to all other property. We have followed this course as regards Cuba and Porto Rico; but, apart from taking the Philippines and continuing to own them, we have made no adjustment of their case. The property, as such, has been administered, and, on the whole, well administered; the amount of work done, indeed, is astonishing. But that is not the issue: however good has been the official administration of the Archipelago, whatever the progress under our tutelage of its peoples as a whole, no one knows to-day what relation will be permanently established between the Archipelago and the United States, what our policy is, or is to be, in respect of the Islands. And yet upon our declaration of a policy hangs their future. The matter in its interest and importance is national; equally national is the indifference we have displayed with respect to its settlement. Both the United States and the Philippines are entitled to a decision.

SECTION II

II.

At the outset of any consideration of the question in hand, it is obvious that we are not shut up *a priori* to any one solution. Thus, we may decide, to keep the Islands, or we may grant them immediate independence, or independence at some future date; we may establish a protectorate, or give a qualified independence, or even turn them over to some other power - for example, England or Japan; or, finally, we may secure an international agreement to neutralize the Islands, thus ostensibly guarding them against the ambitions of powerful neighbors of colonizing disposition. All of these solutions have at one time or another been mentioned; not one of them has ever been officially announced by the Government, or ratified by the people. Although they are all possible, yet a moment's thought shows that they are of very different weight: it is hard to conceive, for example, of our turning the Islands over to England. Excluding, then, cession to any foreign power, we may roughly arrange the various possibilities in a scale, as it were: (*a*) absolute retention; (*b*) qualified retention; (*c*) protectorate; (*d*) neutralization; (*e*) international indepen-dence at some future date; (*f*) immediate international independence. On examining this list thus arranged, certain deductions appear. The stated various possibilities are not all independent, nor are they all exclusive one of the others. Thus (*a*) excludes all the rest, or, better, implies (*b*), (*c*), and (*d*), and excludes (*a*) and (*f*); (*b*) and (*c*) between them are not independent, since a qualified retention may pass into a protectorate. Neutralization not impossibly may ultimately call for a protectorate. Future, independence, so long as unaccomplished, implies (*a*), (*b*), (*c*), and (*d*), while (*f*) is completely exclusive. It may, however, not prevent foreign absorption, if, once out, we stay out.

We shall not here take up all of these possibilities. Whatever other conclusion may be reached, the American people must first pass, either tacitly or explicitly, on retention or independence. If either of these extreme be selected, the other possibilities go by the board. If both are rejected, the remaining four will then have their day in court.

Our immediate purpose, then, is to discuss the question with which this investigation opens, with the definite purpose of suggesting, if not of reaching, conclusions that may help others in forming a decision. It is only when individual decisions have so increased in number as in some sort to form a body of public opinion that future action, whether for or against independence, is to be expected.

SECTION III

III.

However unjustly the American people may treat its own self in respect of tariffs and other issues deeply affecting its welfare, it may be taken for granted, and is so taken here, that in foreign relations the desire of the people is to do what is right. The right determined, a duty is imposed. Clearly, then, we must first try to discover in this case what is right - what is right for us, what is right for the Islanders. It may be that what is theoretically right, or regarded as theoretically right, shall turn out to be practically wrong; or that what is right for the one shall be wrong for the other. Again, some common standing-ground may be found, where the right of each, converted into the rights of both, may so far overlap as substantially to coincide.

The idea is held by a vigorous few, and incessantly expressed, that the American people, through force of arms, is holding in subjection and depriving of liberty another people; that this state of affairs is wrong, bad for both sides, and should come to an end by an immediate grant of full independence to the Filipino people, because no one nation is good enough to hold any other in subjection. It is pertinent to remark, that these ideas so far have found no nation-wide expression: as already said, they are the expression of only a few, but they may be the private opinions of many.

Taken together, they constitute what may be called the purely abstract view of the case. This view takes no account of attendant conditions; it asserts that the right is one and only one thing, and can not be anything else; that is to say, it defines the right and refuses to admit that any other definition will hold, or that any elements can enter into the definition other than those which it has seen fit to include. If no other aspect of the case be correct, our duty is indeed plain. But it is conceivable that this view may not be correct, or at least that so many other factors have to be considered that what might be true in the abstract is subject to very considerable modification when applied to things as they are.

Of this, no better illustration can be given here than the error committed when it is asserted that we, one people, are holding another people, the Filipino, in subjection. As a matter of fact, there is no Filipino people. A certain number of persons, about eight millions, inhabit, the Philippine Archipelago, but it is no more correct to call these one people than it is to call the Europeans one people, because they happen to inhabit the European continent. It is well to keep this point in mind, because, unless a grave error is here committed, the impression prevails that it is one single, homogeneous people whom we are unjustly depriving of independence. At any rate, if not categorically expressed, the connotation of the idea of homogeneity exists. How far this is from the truth is so evident to any person having the slightest real acquaintance with the Philippines, that it would hardly be worth while to dwell upon the matter here, were it not for the ignorance of our people at large. It is convenient to speak of the Filipino people, just as it is convenient to speak of the Danish people, or of the English; but

Cornelis De Witt Willcox

whereas, when we say "Danish" or "English" we mean one definite thing that exists as such, when we say "Filipino" we should understand that the term stands for a relatively great number of very different things. For example, confining ourselves for the moment to the Christianized tribes, it may be asserted that the inhabitants of the great Cagayan Valley, the tobacco-growing country, are at least as different from those of the Visayas, the great middle group of Islands, as are the Italians from the Spanish. Precisely similar differences, increasing, roughly, with the difference of latitude, may be drawn almost at random between any other pairs of the elements constituting the Filipino population. The Ilokanos, to give only one more illustration, have almost nothing more, in common with the Bicols than the fact that they both probably come from the same original stock, just as the English and the Germans have the same ancestors. All these subdivisions speak different languages, and the vast majority do not speak Spanish at all.

But this is not all. The Filipino peoples are divided into two great classes, the Christian and the non-Christian. Now, these non-Christians number over a million, and are themselves broken up into many subdivisions, not only differing in language, customs, habits and traditions, but until very recently bitterly hostile to one another, and so low in the scale of political development that, unlike our own Indians, they have never risen to any conception of even tribal government or organization. Moreover, in Moroland, in the great island of Mindanao with its neighbors, the situation is further complicated by the fact that the dominant elements are Mohammedan. Over most of these non-Christians the Spaniards had not even the shadow of control. The appellation "Filipino people" is therefore wholly erroneous; more than that, it is even dangerously fallacious, in that its use blinds or tends to blind our own people to the real conditions existing in the Archipelago. It is correct to speak of the Filipino *peoples*, because this expression is, geographically, accurately descriptive; but it is absolutely misleading to speak of the Filipino *people*, because of the false political idea involved and conveyed by the use of the singular number. Similarly, there is no objection to the term "Filipino" or "Filipinos," so long as we understand it to mean merely an inhabitant or the inhabitants of the Philippine Archipelago, more narrowly the Christianized inhabitant or inhabitants; but it is distinctly wrong to give to the term a political or national color. It may be remarked now that the divisions, both Christian and non-Christian, of which we have been speaking, determined as they are by natural conditions, are likely to survive for many generations to come. At any rate, the fact that many, and those the most important, constituent elements of the proposed independent government are widely separated by the seas, and that even those situated on the same islands are confined by mountain ranges hitherto extremely difficult to cross, makes it plain that the homogeneity necessary to the formation and permanency of a strong government will be hard to secure, or, if ever secured, to maintain.

When, therefore, it is proposed to grant independence to the Philippine Islands, let it be recollected that this grant is to be made not to a single homogeneous people, of one speech, of one religion, of one state of civilization, of one degree of social and political development, but to an aggregation of peoples, of different speech, of different religions, of widely varying states of social and political development, of little or no communication with one another - to an aggregation, in short, whose elements, before 1898, had had but one bond, the involuntary bond of inherited subjection to Spanish authority, and all of which to-day are distinguished by the characteristic trait of the Oriental, absence of the quality of sympathy.

SECTION VI

IV.

Since, at international law, our title to the Islands is unclouded, it follows that our responsibility in the premises is complete. If, therefore, in the administration of our responsibility, our wards should make a request for independence, it is our duty to examine this request, to inquire into its origin, and then to investigate its reasonableness with the purpose of determining whether, in the circumstances, our wards are able, prepared, or ready to undertake the responsibilities which they pray us to discharge upon them.

That the request for independence is made, and frequently made, there can be no doubt. It has been made in the past and it will continue to be made in the future. One hears it in speeches, and the native press echoes it. Regularly the Assembly closes, or used to close, its sessions by a resolution calling upon the United States to grant immediate independence to the Philippine Islands. Apparently the request has some volume; in any case, it is more or less loudly made. Now, if the demand is widespread, if it conies from all ranks of society, from the humblest peasant in the rice-paddies to the richest merchant of Manila, from the tobacco-planter of the Cagayan Valley to the hemp-stripper of Davao, if it is made in full recognition of the responsibilities involved, then, whether we are disposed to grant it or not, it is a serious matter. It becomes serious, objectively, because so many people arc asking for it. Even if the demand come but from a few, the matter is nevertheless, subjectively, one of concern, because we are responsible, and no factor or element should be overlooked in making up our minds.

Now, it is a fact that the chief demand for independence comes from the Tagalogs, the subdivision or tribe of the Filipinos (we are using the word here and elsewhere as a convenience merely) inhabiting Manila and the adjacent provinces. We speak in all kindliness when we say that they are distinguished by a certain restlessness of disposition, by a considerable degree of vanity. They are not so given to labor as some others - for example, the Ilokanos, to whom they are measurably inferior in point of trustworthiness. More numerous than any other tribe except the Visayans, they are also wealthier and better educated. Some of them have therefore earned and achieved distinction, but these are exceptions, for in general they are characterized by volatility and superficiality. They are more mixed in blood than other tribes. It is not without significance that it was these same Tagalogs who organized in the past the chief insurrections against the domination of Spain, principally, as is well known, because of the misrule of the friars. It is also a fact that the farther one removes from Manila the feebler becomes the cry for independence. If we consider the condition of the loudest supporters of the movement, we find them all, or nearly all, to be politicians, *politicos*. Some of these politicians are not Tagalogs - for example, Senor Osmena, the Speaker of the Assembly, is a Visayan; so that it would perhaps be more accurate to say of the entire propaganda that it is an affair of the politicians, supported chiefly by

Tagalogs. In other words, it is worth while to ask ourselves if the demand for independence be real, arising out of the necessities of the people, or artificial, exploited by the politicians for ends not unfamiliar to us here in the States. It is useless to appeal for a decision to public opinion in the Archipelago, that shall include the whole population, for no such public opinion exists or can exist. And if it be argued that lack of public opinion is no disproof of the existence of a real desire for independence, the rejoinder springs at once to the tongue, that independence would be a sham where public opinion is impossible. There is cause to believe that the true aspect of the case is to be found in a remark made by a young Tagalog (to Mr. Taft himself, if we recollect aright), that there was no reason why independence should not be established at once, seeing that the two things needed already existed in the Philippines, to-wit, the governed in the shape of the peasantry of the fields, and the governors among the *gente fina,* the *gente ilustrada* (the superior classes) of Manila. However this may be, a native newspaper of Manila, distinguished by its hostility to all things American, by its insistent demand for independence, did not hesitate to accuse the wealthy Filipino class of being "refractory to the spirit of association," of being "egotistical and disdainful toward the middle and lower classes," and of refusing "to join their interests with those of the lower classes." [53]

We do not go so far as do some, and believe that the whole agitation is but a conspiracy to place the destinies of the Islands in the hands of an oligarchy. But, in all probability, a Tagalog oligarchy would be formed; for the capital, Manila, is Tagalog, the adjacent provinces are Tagalog, the wealthy class of the Islands on the whole is Tagalog, and there is no middle class anywhere. The mere fact that the capital is situated in the Tagalog provinces would perhaps alone determine the issue, apart from the fact that the Tagalogs are the dominant element, of the native population. Before granting independence, therefore, we should be reasonably sure that we are not in reality placing supreme control in the hands of a few.

But let us suppose that in fact the populations of the Archipelago were quite generally to ask for independence. We must again ask ourselves, How genuine or real would this demand be? It is not very difficult to answer this question. The Filipino is most easily led and influenced; indeed, it is to be doubted if anywhere else in the world a being can be found more easily led and influenced. [54] For example, it is relatively not an uncommon thing, certainly in the Tagalog provinces, for a man having a grudge against a neighbor to invite three or four friends to join him in boloing his enemy. The invitation is frequently accepted, although the guests may themselves have nothing whatever against the victim-to-be. Early in 1909, a miscreant who had been parading himself in women's clothes as a female Jesus Christ, upon exposure by a native doctor, out of revenge got together a band of nineteen men, and with their help proceeded to cut the doctor to pieces. This occurred within a day's march of Manila. The example just given suggests another Filipino trait, the readiness with which the more ignorant will swallow any and all religious nostrums, and form absurd sects, usually for the financial or other material benefit of their leaders. In yet another case, a murderous bandit [55] of Tayabas Province, a Tagalog province, whom we caught and very properly hanged, used to promise as a reward for any deed of special villainy in which he might be interested, a bit of *independencia* (independence), and then would show a box with the word painted on it, declaring that it contained a supply sent down to him from Manila. He never failed to find men to do his will. Our purpose in citing these examples, whose number might be indefinitely multiplied, is not to show that the poor, ignorant Filipino is especially criminal of disposition, but to point out the ease with which he can be led by other men. If, under evil influence, he will altruistically, as it were, consent to almost any crime, obviously he can be induced to consent to almost anything else. His consent or acquiescence can not be taken to indicate appreciation of the issue.

If told, then, by his political leaders that he must ask for independence, the Filipino most certainly will ask for it; and the fact that in the majority of cases he has no idea of what he is asking for will make no difference to him, just as this makes no difference to his *cacique*, or boss. But it ought to make a great deal of difference to us. We may be giving him edged tools to play with, only to find when too late that the edge has been turned against him, a result for which we should then be directly responsible. If a general or universal request could be taken to show that lack of independence is operating to deprive the Filipino of his liberty and to estop him in the pursuit of happiness, the situation of affairs would be confessedly acute. But it is a fact patent to all who know the country, that the Filipino enjoys a freedom at least as great as that of the average American citizen, and is at complete liberty to pursue happiness in any way consistent with the law of the land and with the rights of others. We must conclude that a request, even if universal, would not necessarily be for us a safe guide of action. The universality shown might prove merely that all had

Cornelis De Witt Willcox

agreed to what had been proposed by the leaders, and would leave untouched the merits of the case.

SECTION V

V.

Intimately allied with this question of reasonableness are those of readiness, preparedness, capacity to assume the burdens as well as the rights and privileges of independence.

On readiness, we need not dwell; it is the readiness of acquiescence, not of preparation: the Filipinos are ready, just as children are ready to play with matches. But preparedness and capacity call for more consideration, however brief.

No one will pretend that the Filipinos have had any political training. Before the arrival of the Spaniards, only 350 years ago, they were all uncivilized. Many of them are still semi-savages; others are savages pure and simple. These facts are indisputable. If, then, we turn to history for assistance, we can not find a single instance of any real political evolution in any of the various divisions of the inhabitants of the Archipelago. The exception furnished by the debased Mohammedan sultanates of the great Island of Mindanao is only apparent. The germ of fruitful growth is everywhere missing. Now, the Spaniards assuredly took no steps to teach their new subjects the art and science of government; there was every reason, from their point of view, why they should not teach this art and science.

On the other hand, our own course has been totally different. We have lost no time in putting political power into the hands of the natives, so that to-day, after fourteen years' possession, municipal and provincial government are almost wholly native. To crown all, we have given the Filipinos an elective legislature, an Assembly, all the members of which are native. Students of the subject at first hand, impartial observers on the spot, declare freely that we have gone much too fast, and that we have granted a measure of political administration and government beyond the native power of assimilation and digestion. With this opinion, sound though it be, we are not immediately concerned: the point we wish to bring out is that the experiment we have made is not free; that the case is one of constrained motion, since everyone knows that the mighty power of the United States dominates the entire situation, and that under these conditions the Filipinos have been exercising themselves in the form of government, rather than in responsible government itself. The Filipino government as such has faced no crisis: behind its treasury stands that of the metropolis. Order is assured by the garrison maintained by us, internal police by the Constabulary, another agency of American origin. But, even if all this were not true, it is questionable if an experience of only eight or nine years affords sufficient ground for the belief that a nascent government could exist and advance under its own power alone.

Our training, ample and generous though it may have been, as it has not, for lack of time if for no other reason, prepared the native to govern himself, so it furnishes no real test of his capacity to govern himself. Self-government is not a function of the mere ability to fill certain offices, to discharge certain routine duties of administration: it depends for its existence and maintenance on the possession of certain qualities, and still more, perhaps, on the possession of those qualities by a majority of the people who practice or are to practice self-government, on an educated and inherited interest of the citizen in the questions affecting his welfare in so far as this is conditioned by government. Tested in this wise, the Filipino breaks down locally; to believe that anything else will happen internationally is to blind one's self to the teaching of experience.

But there is yet another test. If political independence is to be of value to those who have it, if it is to endure in any useful way, it must rest on economic independence. The state must be able to meet its obligations, and by this we do not mean merely its current bills, its housekeeping bills, as it were, but its obligations of all and whatever nature, interior police, finance, administration, dispensation of justice, communications, sanitation, education, defense. We do not find these things too easy in our own land, and all of us can without effort bring to mind examples of independent societies in tropical regions, where, these things being neglected, the resultant government is a mockery. Have we any reason to believe that the Filipino, untrained, inexperienced, occupying an undeveloped area of special configuration in a region where continuous effort is disagreeable and initiative distressing, will achieve success where others of greater original fitness have made a failure?

Evidently the possibility of obtaining an answer to this question depends on the possibility of determining, within allowable limits of precision, the qualities and defects of the Filipino peoples. Now, this is a difficult thing to do, but it is not an impossible thing; at any rate, a first approximation may be derived from the authorities quoted in the "Census of the Philippine Islands," 1903, pp 492 *et seq.* In time, these authorities range from Legaspi, 1565, to our own day, and include governors, prelates, travellers, engineers, priests, etc., among whom are found Spaniards, Englishmen, Americans, and Filipinos, As might be expected, all sorts of qualities and defects are reported. Classifying these, and rejecting from consideration all, whether quality or defect, not supported by at least five authorities, it may be concluded, so far as this induction goes, that the Filipino is, on the one hand, hospitable, courageous, fond of music, show, and display; and, on the other, indolent, superstitious, dishonest, and addicted to gambling. One quality, imitativeness, is possibly neutral. It would appear that his virtues do not especially look toward thrift - *i.e.*, economic independence - and that his defects positively look the other way. If the witnesses testifying be challenged on the score of incompetency, let us turn to the reports of the supervisors of the census, contained in the volume already cited; for these cover the entire Archipelago, and set forth actual conditions at one and the same epoch, 1903, the date of the census. Moreover, these supervisors, as welt as the special agents and enumerators, were nearly all natives. When, therefore, these supervisors report the mass of the Christianized Filipinos as simple and superstitious, we may be sure that we have the truth; but we are also inevitably led to the conclusion of economic unfitness. As this matter of economic independence is one of the first importance in determining the future of the Islands, we must look for all the light possible on the question. A flood is thrown on it by an article entitled "*Nulla est Redemptio*," published in the (native) *La Democracia*, of Manila, October 10, 1910, and believed to be the production of perhaps the ablest Filipino alive to-day. Premising that agriculture is the chief source of Philippine wealth, and that this source failing, all others must fail, the author points out that, although taxes are lighter in the Archipelago than in any other country, production is much less, and that this is the chief cause of the prevailing economic distress. He points out further that the Assembly is wholly native, as are all municipal and nearly all provincial officers, and that therefore they, and the constituencies that elected them, must assume responsibility. Now, what has been achieved? The provinces have spent money on buildings and parks, but, with one brilliant exception, none on roads. Nothing has been done for agriculture. Of the municipalities, the least said the better; they are a wreck in the full extension of the word. And, as the hope of a people must rest in its youth, what does he find to be the case? Thousands of candidates in pharmacy, law, medicine; as regards the Civil Service, enough candidates to fill all the posts in the Islands for generations to come. But of farmers, young men willing to return to the fields, their own fields, and by the sweat of their brow to work out the salvation of the country? None: the development of this principal element of national existence is left to the ignorant and indolent peasantry. He draws no less gloomy a picture in respect of capital and property. Nine-tenths of Manila, and all important provincial real estate, is mortgaged. Capital is furnished at exorbitant rates of interest, and usury prevails. In the country, no security is accepted save real property, and then only when the lender is satisfied that his debtor will be unable to pay, and that the security will pass.

Bad as the outlook is, no remedy suggests itself. For, returning to the theme that agriculture is recognized as vital, much energy is spent in discussion, discourses, lectures, in writing articles, in discovering reasons why agriculture does not flourish, but nothing else and nothing more. [56]

The picture may be overdrawn; but it is a Filipino picture, drawn by a Filipino hand. Let us now permit, the native press to speak again on the subject engaging our attention. Thus *Vanguardia* [57] a bitter anti-American sheet, arraigns its wealthy fellow-country-men for lack of initiative and fondness of routine. It accuses them of a willingness to invest in city property, to deposit money in banks, "to make loans at usurious rates, in which they take advantage of the urgent and pressing necessities of their countrymen," but of unwillingness "to engage in agriculture, marine or industrial enterprise"; and says they are "generally lacking in the spirit of progression." According to another native newspaper, the vice of gambling has infected all classes of society, men and women alike, rich and poor, young and old. Here it is almost impossible to overdraw the picture, so widespread is the vice. Let us now couple these statements, drawn from native sources, with the fact that the Christianized tribes, all told, number some 7,000,000; that of these but one-tenth speak Spanish; and that of this tenth only a very few are educated in any accepted sense of the word. Repeating here a form of summation already employed in this discussion, let us bear in mind that, if we decide to make a grant of independence, we shall be deciding to grant it to a population, composed, first, of a very few educated persons; next, of a small fraction able, through the possession of Spanish, to communicate, with one another; and, lastly, of a remainder - the vast, the immense majority - not only unable so to communicate, but characterized by qualities that, however commendable in themselves, do not constitute a foundation on which popular self-government may safely rest. Further, we mean to grant it to a population which contains no middle class, to one in which the poor are peculiarly at the mercy of the rich, and in which nearly all the elements that make for economic independence are conspicuously lacking.

SECTION VI

VI.

What would happen if we were to grant immediate independence to the Islands? Without having the gift of prophecy, one runs no risk in declaring that civil war would be almost unavoidable. At least this is the belief of some well-informed Filipinos, a belief that appears to have some ground when we take into account, the great probability of a Tagalog oligarchy. But, without going so far as to predict armed strife, it would seem that any government, not held together by some strong external power, would soon begin to break up. Its various elements, not only differentiated from one another by speech, but physically separated, in many cases, by the seas, would tend to fall apart. The Visayas, for example, would refuse sooner or later to acknowledge the Tagalog supremacy of Luzon. If we proceed farther south still, what practicable bond can be found to exist between Mindanao, peopled by Mohammedans and savages, and Luzon or Panay or Negros? The consequences of such a disruption as is here predicted must occur to everyone. The gravest of these, gravest in that it would defeat our purpose in granting independence, would be foreign intervention. Japan would most certainly insist on being heard. Now, the Filipinos, as a whole, prefer our sovereignty to that of the Japanese. England, too, would have a right to interfere for the protection of her commercial interests in the Archipelago. It exercised this sort of right, in 1882, by seizing Egypt in behalf of civilization in general. In the meantime, the Moros of Mindanao and Jolo would have resumed their piratical excursions to the northward, burning, killing, and carrying off slaves. If this be questioned, then let us recollect that as recently as 1897 they carried off slaves from the Visayas, a sporadic case, probably, but giving evidence that the disease of piracy is to-day merely latent. Given an opportunity, it will break out again. Under independence, the large, beautiful, and fertile island of Mindanao would be left to its own devices, would be lost to civilization. Upon this point we need have no doubt whatever. The issue of Filipino control of Mindanao was very clearly raised, when Mr. Dickinson, the late Secretary of War, visited Mindanao in August of 1910. Upon this occasion Mr. Dickinson, in response to a Filipino plea for immediate independence, with consequent control of the Moros, made a speech in which he declared the unwillingness of the Government to entrust to the 66,000 Filipinos living in Mindanao the government of the 350,000 Moros of this province. At the close of this speech, four *datus* (chiefs), present with 2,000 of their people, and controlling the destinies of 40,000 souls, swore allegiance to the United States; and, requesting that, if the Americans ever withdrew from Mindanao, the Moros should be placed in control, firmly announced, at the same time, their intention to fight if the Americans should ever take their departure. One of the *datus*, Mandi by name, was outspoken in praise of the present Government, and both he and the other chiefs declared that they were contented with things as they are. Such testimony as is afforded by the foregoing incident is not lightly to be brushed aside to make way for an abstraction. If disregarded, then the efforts that we have made to better the condition of Mindanao, to introduce some idea of law and order, some notion of the value of peace and of industry, will come to a sudden end; for the Christianized Filipinos can never hope to cope with the active, warlike pirates of Moroland. So far as this part of the Archipelago is concerned, a grant of independence means the re-establishment of slavery, the recrudescence of piracy, [58] the reincarnation of barbarism. How great a pity this would be may be inferred from the fact that Mindanao forms nearly one-third of the Archipelago in area, and exceeds Java in arable land. Now, Java supports a population of over 25,000,000.

If we turn our attention to the other non-Christian elements of the Islands, the case is no better. The Christianized Filipino fears and dreads the pagan mountaineers, the head-hunters who occupy so large a part of Luzon, the largest and most important island of the Archipelago. He grudges every *centavo* spent under our direction for the betterment of these truly admirable wild men The governor, the Christian governor, of a province bordering on the wild men's territory, had, indeed, no other idea of the way to treat his pagan neighbors, about 50,000 in number, than to kill them all. His argument was that they were worse than useless, why spend any money on them, when, by exterminating them, all questions affecting them would be forever answered? But, under our administration, some excellent work has been done, and is growing, to turn these as yet unspoiled peoples to account in the destinies of the Archipelago. Independence would mean the *end* of this work, the restoration of the old order of rapine, murder, and all injustice as between Christians and pagans, and of internecine strife and warfare as between the communities of the pagans themselves. That this result would follow is not even questioned by those who have acquired their knowledge at first hand. Are we willing to shoulder the responsibility of such a result?

We have at our very doors an example of the danger of independence to a people unfilled for the burdens and responsibilities of self-government. We have already since 1900 been compelled once to intervene in the affairs of Cuba: the possibility of a fresh intervention continually stares our statesmen in the face. But Cuba, let it be observed, in contrast with the Philippines, has but one language, one religion; it has no wild tribes, no Mohammedans; its provinces are not separated from one another by seas of difficult navigation, are bound together by suitable communications. The curse of Cuba is personal politics: have we any assurance that this same curse in a worse form would not come to blast the Philippines?

SECTION VII

VII.

Some of the conclusions reached or hinted at in the course of this argument must have formed themselves in the minds of at least a few Filipinos of independent character. Otherwise how shall we account for the fact that some declare their disbelief in the possibility of independence? How else shall we explain what is far more significant, the silence under this head of the really first-rate men of the Archipelago? Is it not worthy of note that Rizal himself, the posthumous apostle of the Philippines, never advocated or contemplated independence? In yet other cases, the belief held finds expression in the assertion that the Islands must be declared independent, but only under the protection of the United States. What that would ultimately mean is so plain to those who know the country as to require no consideration here. It may even be asserted on the best of authority, so far as any authority is possible in such a case, that not even those who shout the loudest for independence arc sincere in their clamor the Assembly itself would be seriously disturbed if its resolution to this end should suddenly be honored by the United States.

We make bold to quote here, in full, a short editorial that appeared in the *Weekly Times of* Manila, December 30, 1910:

"Mr. Perry Robinson, whose articles on the Philippines are now being published by the London *Times*, makes one point that offers a valuable, suggestion to our ardent friends of the Nationalist party. [59] While here, Mr. Robinson interviewed a number of the leaders of the party and discovered that they were all afraid of immediate independence. They admitted that the country and people would not be ready for it for years, and, when pressed for an explanation, said they feared, if they did not press the question now, it would not avail them to do so later on. The inconsistency of the present position must strike every sensible person who examines it. Let us assume that the United States Government decides at this time to give ear to the plea of those who are politically active in the Philippines - what will happen? It will dispatch a commission or committee to the Islands to examine the representations of those who make the plea. It is admitted by even the Nationalist leaders, when speaking privately on this question, that the people are not ready to shift for themselves and can not be made ready for some years. Surely it is not believed that the investigators are going to be deceived about the real truth as to conditions in the Islands, and we are unable to see what good is to be accomplished by having this inquiry made.

"Would it not be infinitely better for the Nationalist and other leaders in this country to squarely face the facts and base all their future operations on the facing of those facts? One difficulty is that they have made a lot of promises and professions to the people that they are incapable of fulfilling, and another is that they have largely aided in deceiving the people themselves as to where they really stand and as to what they are really capable of under present conditions. But to go on means discredit and failure in the end, and a greater work could be done for the country at large by squarely facing the facts. It must be admitted that neither position is especially pleasant. There has been created among the people a vanity of ability and power that will make the blow a hard one; but unless there are Filipino leaders capable of making the people realize the truth about their position, there is really not much hope for them in the future.

"The truth is, that the race must be built up physically and its numbers be enormously increased before it may seriously assume the obligations of statehood; and, for our part, we await the statesman who is prepared to drive this and other important lessons home to the minds and hearts of the people.

"Assurance and pretense serve their purposes on many occasions, but they must be set aside when it comes to the test that will be applied to the plea that Filipino leaders now make with such persistency."

It is maintained that the matter of this short editorial deserves to be as deeply pondered by the people of the United States as by the Filipinos to whom it is specially addressed.

That all this talk of independence, the motions to that end occasionally made in Congress, the circulation of so-called anti-imperialistic literature, have so far endangered the real interests of the Philippines, there can be no reasonable doubt. The independence propaganda prevents, or tends to prevent, recognition of the fact that the Philippines will be greater with the United States than they can ever hope to be standing alone, if so be that they can stand alone at all. It has retarded the development of the Islands and has checked progress. It forces into the background the fact that with an infinitude of work lying before Americans and Filipinos alike, if the Islands are to have their full value in the world's economy, the best way to do this work is for Americans and Filipinos to labor together, each contributing his share to the common result. Upon this safe ground both may stand. "The law of life is labor; the joy of life is accomplishment." But we can not labor if the fruits of our toil may be torn from us; accomplishment is impossible in the face of uncertainty and dissension. If our people have the welfare of the Philippines genuinely at heart, it must thoroughly consider the question of permanent retention; for this course, on the one hand, would not only clear away all misunderstanding, but, on the other, it would meet the real responsibilities of the case. There is no disposition here to burke the fact that these responsibilities are serious, if not onerous; that they call for administrative statesmanship of a very high order. But we should also recognize the fact that these responsibilities are ours, created by us, and that our rejection of them is sure to be followed by consequences disastrous, not to us, but to the Filipinos themselves. If, on the other hand, we accept these responsibilities, then sooner or later Americans and Filipinos together could bend their energies to the development of a country in which they would now have the same interest. And if, under the prevailing uncertainty, so much has already been accomplished in preventing disease, abating epidemics, building roads and bridges, erecting telegraphs and telephones, lighting the coasts, establishing courts of law, equalizing taxation, conserving forests, founding schools and colleges, encouraging commerce and agriculture, what may not unreasonably be expected if all shall feel that the foundations of order, system, and justice are permanent, that life is secure, liberty assured, and the pursuit of happiness possible?

Surely there is significance in the effect at once produced in the sugar-raising islands by the passage of the Payne Bill: idle fields were planted to cane, and the elections took an unmistakable *americanista* trend. There is no better peacemaker than the pay-master. The Assembly, it is true, fulminated against the bill: success, prosperity, contentment under its operation might mean the dissolution of a dream. So they might; but the bill also categorically established the possibility, and more than the possibility, of permanently profitable relations under the aegis of the United States. It might even ultimately greatly reduce, if not entirely destroy, the racial issue. Here is already common ground, limited though it be, on which Americans and Filipinos may and do stand together. If any doubt should exist on this score, we have but to look at Porto Rico, whose total external commerce has grown, in round numbers, from 17 1/2 million dollars in 1901 to 79 millions in 1911. During this same interval that of the Philippines has risen from 53 million to 90 million dollars, nearly 20 millions of the increase being due to the Payne Bill. The population of Porto Rico (census of 1910) is 1,120,000; that of the Philippines, 8,200,000: the area of Porto Rico is 3,606 square miles; that of the Philippines, 128,000 square miles. This comparison is frankly commercial; but thriving commerce means prosperity, and prosperity spells content. After eliminating certain natural and social advantages enjoyed by Porto Rico, and not by the Philippines, the vast economic difference between the two can be accounted for only by the different relation they respectively bear to the United States, a conclusion confirmed by the effect of the Payne Bill.

In the case of one, this relation is defined; in that of the other, undefined. We intend to remain in Porto Rico; we do not know what we shall do with the Philipines.

Cornelis De Witt Willcox

SECTION VIII

VIII.

To conclude, and in part to repeat: when we took over the Philippines, we unquestionably at the same time acquired a burden. Of this burden we can rid ourselves by setting the Islands adrift; or we can declare that we intend to keep the Islands, as we have kept Porto Rico. In the light of the argument hereinbefore submitted, which of these courses appeals to the people of the United States? May we, or may we not, without incurring an accusation of injustice to a dependent population, honestly ask ourselves if actual conditions should not sometimes limit or control the application of an abstract principle? Does our duty in the premises consist or not in merely satisfying such a principle? Is it or is it not possible that practical considerations - and what is practical is not always sordid - may outweigh an abstraction? Is it or is it not conceivably our duty to use our superior knowledge, power and experience to the best advantage of those chiefly concerned, even if these should apparently for a time not agree with us in the application we purpose to make of our knowledge, power, and experience?

NOTES

[1]   See Retana's edition, p. 183, Madrid, 1909.

[2]   It is interesting to note that as late as 1889 General Weyler, then Governor-General of the Archipelago, in establishing various *comandancias*, drew up regula-tions for the treatment of the natives, etc., as remark-able for lenity and good sense as his later measures in Cuba were, whether justly or not, distinguished for severity.

[3]   For an account of the early missions of this order, see the Manila *Libertas* of May 23, 1910.

[4]   Report of the Secretary of the Interior, Philippine Islands, 1910; Washington Government Printing Office, 1911.

[5]   See "Census of the Philippine Islands," Vol. I., p. 453 *et seq.,* for a discussion of the non-Christian tribes.

[6]   Vol. I., p. 60 *et seq.*

[7]   Mr. A.H. Savage Landor, in his "Gems of the East," protests against our practice of boiling water before drinking it, but the experience of others is against him. He was simply fortunate in not being made ill by the natural water.

[8]   An attempt has been made to stock this river with trout, but it has proved a failure. The fish grew and throve, but did not breed.

[9]   This happened on a large scale in the spring, of this year (1912). Landslides having occurred on both banks of the canon, and as luck would have it, at the same point, the waters rose behind the natural dam thus formed to a height of over one hundred feet, and breaking through, scoured the valley in their sweep, completely wiping out the road.

[10]   For a fuller account of Padre Villaverde's labors, see the Manila *Libertas* of May 17, 1910. Villaverde remained at his post until his health broke completely; he set out for Spain, but never reached it, dying August 4, 1897, and being buried at sea a few hours only from Barcelona. The great trail he built reduced the cost of transportation by nine-tenths.

[11]   According to the native legend, this mountain used to form part of the Zambales range. It became, however, by reason of its quarrelsome disposition, so objectionable to its neighbors of this range, that they finally resolved no longer to endure its cantankerousness and accordingly banished it to its present position in the plain of Central Luzon, where it would have no neighbors to annoy, and where it has stood ever since, rising solitary from the surrounding plain.

[12]   Dr. Barrows, in the "Census of the Philippine Islands," Vol. I., p 471, says that the etymology of this word is unknown. As it seems to mean "people of the mountains," it is not unlikely to be a form of "Igolot," by metathesis, as it were.

[13]   According to some accounts, the Highlanders, in throwing the spear, give it a rotation around its longest axis, twirling it rapidly in the hand as this is brought up before the throw. In other words, they have discovered that a rotating spear has greater accuracy than a non-rotating one. If this is true, this discovery is worthy to be bracketed with the use of the fire-syringe by the Tinguians of the North, and by certain other wild people of the Archipelago.

[14]   These salt deposits are now (1912), to the great satisfaction of the people of the province, being worked by the Government, and salt has ceased to be a luxury within the reach of only the few rich.

[15]   The Ilongots are so few in number and scattered over so vast and rough a country that trail-making can never be as successful in their territory as it has been farther north.

[16]   Dampier's description of what he saw in Mindanao fits here: "This Distemper runs with a dry Scurf all over their Bodies, and causeth great itching in those that have it, making them frequently scratch and scrub themselves, which raiseth the outer skin in small whitish flakes, like the scales of little Fish, when they are raised on end with a Knife. This makes their skin extraordinary rough, and in some you shall see broad white spots in several parts of their Body. I judge such have had it, but are cured; for their skins were smooth, and I did not perceive them to scrub themselves: yet I have learnt from their own mouths that these spots were from this Distemper." - Dampier's "Voyages," Masefield's edition, p. 341; New York, E. P. Dutton & Co., 1906.

[17]   On one of his first expeditions elsewhere, however, when the women realized that they were really to receive gifts of beads, etc., they rushed Mr. Worcester and his assistants, upsetting them all in their eagerness to get at the stuff.

[18]   So Strong said, himself an accomplished violinist.

[19]   The straw mat covering the "split bottom" of the native bed. There is no other mattress, and the "split bottom" constitutes the springs. Once accustomed to it, the bed is cool and comfortable.

[20]   Dampier's "Voyages," p. 319, Masefield's edition.

[21]   According to De Morga (p. 196, Retana's edition), the *anito* was a representation of the devil under horrible and frightful forms, to which fruits and fowl and perfumes were offered. Each house had and "made" (or performed) its *anitos*, there being no temples, without ceremony or any special solemnity. "This word," says Retana, "is ordinarily interpreted 'idol,' although it has other meanings. There were *anitos* of the mountains, of the fields, of the sea. The soul of an ancestor, according to some, became embodied as a new *anito*, hence the expression, 'to make *anitos*. Even living beings, notably the crocodile, were regarded as *anitos* and worshiped. The *anito-figura*, generally shortened to *anito*, ... was usually a figurine of wood, though sometimes of gold." (Glossary to his edition of De Morga, pp. 486-487.)

"The *anito* of the Philippines is essentially a protecting spirit." (F. Jagor, "Travels in the Philippines," p. 298.

English translation, London, Chapman & Hall, 1875; originally published in Berlin. 1873, "Reisen in den Philippinen," Weidmannsche Buchhandlung.)

"The religion of the islands, what may be called the true religion of Filipinos, consisted of the worship of the *anitos*. These were not gods, but the souls of departed ancestors, and each family worshipped its own, in order to obtain their favorable influence." (Pardo de Tavera, "Resena Historica de Filipinas," Manila, 1906.)

[22]   *Apo* means "lord, master." In the mountains every American is called *apo*. "Sir" in Tagalo is *po*, and the highest mountain of the Archipelago is named Apo. The native word for fire in these parts is something like *apo*. To distinguish Mr. Forbes from other *apos*. he was called *apo apo* in communicating with the natives.

[23]   Now frequently called *ub-ub, i.e.,* "spring," in the Ifugao country; a change of name due to Gallman.

[24]   See De Morga, "*Sucesos*," etc., p. 184, Retana's edition, and Retana's note on the passage; see also Jagor, "Travels," etc., p. 162 *et seq*.

[25]   *Runo* is a stiff reed grass growing to several feet, the mountain cousin of the *cogon* of the plains.

[26]   The *Princesa* was the only fat person we saw in the mountains: apparently these Highlanders all grow thin with age, and wrinkled from head to foot.

[27]   See *Philippine Journal of Science*, July, 1909, for Villaverde's account of the Ifugaos of Kiangan,

translated and edited by Worcester, with notes and an addendum by Major Case, of the Constabulary.

[28]   Gallman says they also carry their spears point down to cause the enemy's spears to miss. - *C. De W.W.*

[29]   As a matter of fact, they were "the terror of the Spaniards"; they "annihilated an entire garrison at Payoan," "exacted a heavy annual toll of heads from the people of Ragabag, and ... made the main trail from Nueva Vizcaya to Isabela so dangerous that three strong garrisons were constantly maintained on it, and ... people were not allowed to travel over it: except under military escort, and even so were often attacked and killed." (Worcester, *The National Geographic Magazine*, March, 1911.) Gallman's mere name now suffices to do what three strong Spanish garrisons failed to do.

[30]   This danger still exists in the case of the savages of the Southern Islands of the Archipelago, but Mr. Worcester, if undisturbed, will bring these in too, all in time. In the fall of this very year, 1910, his party was attacked in Palawan.

[31]   Many years ago some Moros were brought to Mayoyao to work tobacco. The Ifugaos deeply resenting this invasion, at the first opportunity attacked and killed them all. Only one woman escaped, covered with wounds, to Echaguee, where she was in 1910, still alive. The fight was most desperate, three Ifugaos biting the dust for every Moro killed.

[32]   See a native account of the part played by the Igorots in this battle, in Seidenadel's "The First

Grammar of the Language Spoken by the Bontoc Igorot"; Chicago, Open Court Publishing Company, 1909.

[33]   Sometimes also called the Caicayan.

[34]   Samoki is celebrated for its pottery, sold all through this region, and of such quality that the Igorots use vessels made here to reduce copper ore. The potter's wheel is unknown. In regard to the skill of the highlanders in metallurgy, see Jagor, "Travels," p. 181.

[35]   So do their cousins of Formosa. Pickering, "Pioneering in Formosa," p. 150; London, Hurst & Blackett, 1898.

[36]   For a full account of the way in which the Igorots have taken to our sports, see Mr. Worcester's article in the March, 1911, number of the *National Geographic Magazine.*

[37]   A similiar institution exists among the aborigines of Formosa. "... the unmarried men and boys slept in a shed raised from the ground. This building was regarded as a kind of temple, in which the vanquished heads were hung." (Pickering, "Pioneering in Formosa," p. 148.)

[38]   For a more or less complete account of the Bontok Igorot, see Jenks's "The Bontoc Igorot"; Manila, Bureau of Public Printing, 1905. For the language, consult "The First Grammar of the Language Spoken by the Bontoc Igorot," by Doctor Carl Wilhelm Seidenadel; Chicago, Open Court Publishing Company, 1909.

[39]   Dampier mentions this drink in his "New Voyage Around the World." He calls it *bashee*, and found it in the Batanes Islands, just north of Luzon: "And indeed, from the plenty of this Liquor, and their plentiful use of it, our Men call'd all these Islands, the Bashee Islands." (Masefield's edition, p. 425.)

[40]   De La Gironiere, in his "Aventures d'un Gentilhomme Breton aux Iles Philippines," describes (Chapter V.) a feast, at which he had, while on a visit to the Tinguianes, to drink human brains mixed with *basi*. Whatever De La Gironiere says must be received with considerable caution; but Pickering, a prosaic and matter-of-fact Britisher, speaking of the Formosan savages, says that "they mixed the brains of their enemies with wine." ("Pioneering in Formosa," p. 153).

[41]   For example, this year (1912) more people "came in" to meet Mr. Worcester then ever before. In Bontok every valley of the sub-province was represented, and there was a time when representatives of all the villages danced together on the plaza, an event of importance in the history of these people as marking the passing of old feuds and a determination to live at piece with one another. A moving picture machine was taken along in a four-wheeled wagon (showing incidentally that the main trails have become roads since 1910), and created both enthusiasm and alarm: enthusiasm when some familiar scene with known living persons was thrown upon the screen, and alarm when a railway train, for example, was shown advancing upon the spectators, causing many of them to flee for safety to the neighboring hills and woods.

[42]   For an account of what this Government

monopoly really meant, see Jagor, "Travels," etc., p. 324. A Spaniard of my acquaintance told me that if a native's attention to his crop did not please the inspectors, they would cause him to be publicly flogged on Sunday before the church after mass; and if this course brought no amendment, they would then cut his stand down. Jagor, who travelled in the Philippines as long ago as 1859-60, could see no future for them save under American control, and he predicted that this control would come, an astonishing prophecy. "In proportion as the navigation of the west coast of America extends the influence of the American element over the South Sea, the captivating, magic power which the great Republic exercises over the Spanish colonies will not fail to make itself felt also in the Philippines. The Americans are evidently destined to bring to a full development the germs originated by the Spaniards." ("Travels in the Philippines," p. 369.) Jagor's work, it may be remarked, will always remain an authority on the Philippines.

[43]   The cable and popular name of the "Compania General de Tabacos de Filipinas"; it owns plantations up the Grande in Isabela Province.

[44]   So do the aborigines of Formosa. "These aborigines of the hills live in villages. Their houses are built, of stone, roofed with slate, and have a remarkably clean, home-like appearance." (Pickering, "Pioneering in Formosa," p. 69.)

[45]   The word "Filipino" is taken to mean the civilized, Christianized inhabitant of Malay origin of the Philippine Islands. As such, it is convenient and useful. It should be recollected, however, that there is

no such thing as a *Filipino people*. There are Tagalogs, Visayans, Bicols, Pampangans, Ilokanos, Cagayanes, etc., etc., to say nothing of the wild people themselves, all speaking different languages; but these can not be said to form one people.

[46]   Retana, in his edition (1909) of De Morga remarks (p. 502): "To-day there would not be many to dare go from Manila to Aparri by the road taken by the Spaniards in 1591."

[47]   Some Igorots brought down to the Manila carnival of 1912 were forced, at the request of Filipino authorities, to put on trousers. This was not for comfort's sake, nor yet for decency's, for the bare human skin is no uncommon sight in Manila. Apparently, the Filipinos of Manila were unwilling to let the world note that their cousins of the mountains were still in the naked state.

[48]   For a full discussion of this entire matter, see the Report of the Secretary of the Interior, Philippine Islands, for 1910, Washington Government Printing Office, 1911, from which the quotations given above are taken.

[49]   E.g. the Mountain Province. - C. De W.W.

[50]   It is interesting to note, that since the foregoing report was published, Captain Harris, Philippine Constabulary, has persuaded the Kalingas to turn in one hundred and eighty-seven firearms in their possession, and this without firing a shot himself. What this means may be inferred from the fact that all over the Islands, whether among Christians or non-Christians, the desire to have firearms is of the keenest.

The great ambition of the Ifugao is to be a policeman, and so be authorized to carry a gun. The Moros will give $400.00 for an Army rifle and a belt of ammunition worth, say, $18.00. - C. De W.W.

[51] *Japan Chronicle*, weekly edition, Kobe, January 5, 1911.

[52] Ibid., same date.

[53] See the weekly Manila *Times*, October 21, 1910.

[54] According to a story current some years ago, a distinguished officer of our Army serving in the Philippines once remarked to a justly celebrated native judge of the highest character, that he had no opinion of the native justice, and added, that for a thousand pesos he could procure witnesses to prove that the judge had committed a murder in such a place, although the judge had never been in the place in his life. "Absurd," remarked the judge. "How absurd?" "You misunderstand me," answered the judge; "it would be absurd to spend a thousand pesos on such a purpose when two hundred would suffice."

[55] This worthy, Ruperto Rios by name, in succession promoted himself to brigadier and major general, and then announced himself as generalissimo. As though this were not enough, he next proclaimed himself pope, "Papa Rios," and then crowned his earthly glories by calling himself Jesus Christ, and as such was hanged. Our pity for such sell-delusion is tempered by the fact that the purpose in view was crime.

[56]   It is only fair to remark that the Government is doing every thing in its power to develop native interest in agriculture. Of course it is too early as yet to say whether its efforts will be rewarded.

[57]   Quoted in the weekly Manila *Times* of October 21, 1910.

[58]   That piracy, even under our strong control is not dead is shown by the following:

"*Manila*, April 15. A pirate raid, is reported trom Jolo, where a Japanese pearl-fishing bout was found adrift and looted. The crew of the pearler are missing, and are believed to be murdered. The Mataja Lighthouse has also been attacked and robbed, presumably by the same band. Gunboats have been sent to investigate." New York *Times*, April 15, 1912.

[59]   The party of immediate independence.

Choose from Thousands of 1stWorldLibrary Classics By

Adolphus WilliamWard
Aesop
Agatha Christie
Alexander Aaronsohn
Alexander Kielland
Alexandre Dumas
Alfred Gatty
Alfred Ollivant
Alice Duer Miller
Alice Turner Curtis
Alice Dunbar
Ambrose Bierce
Amelia E. Barr
Andrew Lang
Andrew McFarland Davis
Anna Sewell
Annie Besant
Annie Hamilton Donnell
Annie Payson Call
Anton Chekhov
Arnold Bennett
Arthur Conan Doyle
Arthur Ransome
Atticus
B. M. Bower
Basil King
Bayard Taylor
Ben Macomber
Booth Tarkington
Bram Stoker
C. Collodi
C. E. Orr
C. M. Ingleby
Carolyn Wells
Catherine Parr Traill
Charles A. Eastman
Charles Dickens
Charles Dudley Warner
Charles Farrar Browne
Charles Ives
Charles Kingsley
Charles Lathrop Pack
Charles Whibley
Charles Willing Beale
Charlotte M. Braeme
Charlotte M.Yonge
Clair W. Hayes
Clarence Day Jr.
Clarence E. Mulford

Clemence Housman
Confucius
Cornelis DeWitt Wilcox
Cyril Burleigh
D. H. Lawrence
Daniel Defoe
David Garnett
Don Carlos Janes
Donald Keyhole
Dorothy Kilner
Dougan Clark
E. Nesbit
E.P.Roe
E. Phillips Oppenheim
Edgar Allan Poe
Edgar Rice Burroughs
Edith Wharton
Edward J. O'Biren
John Cournos
Edwin L. Arnold
Eleanor Atkins
Elizabeth Cleghorn
Gaskell
Elizabeth Von Arnim
Ellem Key
Emily Dickinson
Erasmus W. Jones
Ernie Howard Pie
Ethel Turner
Ethel Watts Mumford
Eugenie Foa
Eugene Wood
Evelyn Everett-Green
Everard Cotes
F. J. Cross
Federick Austin Ogg
Ferdinand Ossendowski
Francis Bacon
Francis Darwin
Frances Hodgson Burnett
Frank Gee Patchin
Frank Harris
Frank Jewett Mather
Frank L. Packard
Frederick Trevor Hill
Frederick Winslow Taylor
Friedrich Kerst
Friedrich Nietzsche
Fyodor Dostoyevsky

Gabrielle E. Jackson
Garrett P. Serviss
Gaston Leroux
George Ade
Geroge Bernard Shaw
George Ebers
George Eliot
George MacDonald
George Orwell
George Tucker
George W. Cable
George Wharton James
Gertrude Atherton
Grace E. King
Grant Allen
Guillermo A. Sherwell
Gulielma Zollinger
Gustav Flaubert
H. A. Cody
H. B. Irving
H. G. Wells
H. H. Munro
H. Irving Hancock
H. Rider Haggard
H. W. C. Davis
Hamilton Wright Mabie
Hans Christian Andersen
Harold Avery
Harold McGrath
Harriet Beecher Stowe
Harry Houidini
Helent Hunt Jackson
Helen Nicolay
Hendy David Thoreau
Henrik Ibsen
Henry Adams
Henry Ford
Henry Frost
Henry James
Henry Jones Ford
Henry Seton Merriman
Henry Wadsworth
Longfellow
Henry W Longfellow
Herbert A. Giles
Herbert N. Casson
Herman Hesse
Homer
Honore De Balzac

Horace Walpole
Horatio Alger, Jr.
Howard Pyle
Howard R. Garis
Hugh Lofting
Hugh Walpole
Humphry Ward
Ian Maclaren
Israel Abrahams
J.G.Austin
J. Henri Fabre
J. M. Barrie
J. Macdonald Oxley
J. S. Knowles
J. Storer Clouston
Jack London
Jacob Abbott
James Allen
James Lane Allen
James Andrews
James Baldwin
James DeMille
James Joyce
James Oliver Curwood
James Oppenheim
James Otis
Jane Austen
Jens Peter Jacobsen
Jerome K. Jerome
John Burroughs
John F. Kennedy
John Gay
John Glasworthy
John Habberton
John Joy Bell
John Milton
John Philip Sousa
Jonathan Swift
Joseph Carey
Joseph Conrad
Joseph Jacobs
Julian Hawthrone
Julies Vernes
Justin Huntly McCarthy
Kakuzo Okakura
Kenneth Grahame
Kate Langley Bosher
L. A. Abbot
L. T. Meade
L. Frank Baum
Laura Lee Hope

Laurence Housman
Leo Tolstoy
Leonid Andreyev
Lewis Carroll
Lilian Bell
Lloyd Osbourne
Louis Tracy
Louisa May Alcott
Lucy Fitch Perkins
Lucy Maud Montgomery
Lydia Miller Middleton
Lyndon Orr
M. H. Adams
Margaret E. Sangster
Margaret Vandercook
Maria Edgeworth
Maria Thompson Daviess
Mariano Azuela
Marion Polk Angellotti
Mark Overton
Mark Twain
Mary Austin
Mary Cole
Mary Rowlandson
Mary Wollstonecraft
Shelley
Max Beerbohm
Myra Kelly
Nathaniel Hawthrone
O. F. Walton
Oscar Wilde
Owen Johnson
P.G.Wodehouse
Paul and Mable Thorn
Paul G. Tomlinson
Paul Severing
Peter B. Kyne
Plato
R. Derby Holmes
R. L. Stevenson
Rabindranath Tagore
Rahul Alvares
Ralph Waldo Emmerson
Rene Descartes
Rex E. Beach
Richard Harding Davis
Richard Jefferies
Robert Barr
Robert Frost
Robert Gordon Anderson
Robert L. Drake

Robert Lansing
Robert Michael Ballantyne
Robert W. Chambers
Rosa Nouchette Carey
Ross Kay
Rudyard Kipling
Samuel B. Allison
Samuel Hopkins Adams
Sarah Bernhardt
Selma Lagerlof
Sherwood Anderson
Sigmund Freud
Standish O'Grady
Stanley Weyman
Stella Benson
Stephen Crane
Stewart Edward White
Stijn Streuvels
Swami Abhedananda
Swami Parmananda
T. S. Ackland
The Princess Der Ling
Thomas A. Janvier
Thomas A Kempis
Thomas Anderton
Thomas Bailey Aldrich
Thomas Bulfinch
Thomas De Quincey
Thomas H. Huxley
Thomas Hardy
Thomas More
Thornton W. Burgess
U. S. Grant
Valentine Williams
Victor Appleton
Virginia Woolf
Walter Scott
Washington Irving
Wilbur Lawton
Wilkie Collins
Willa Cather
Willard F. Baker
William Makepeace
Thackeray
William W. Walter
Winston Churchill
Yei Theodora Ozaki
Young E. Allison
Zane Grey

www.ingramcontent.com/pod-product-compliance
Lightning Source LLC
Chambersburg PA
CBHW020501100426
42813CB00030B/3071/J